Reviews of Mainak Dhar's *Brand New Start: Fast-Start Your Career with the Power of Personal Branding*
Gold Winner at Non-Fiction Book Awards, 2021

'A lively and very approachable call to readers to manage their own brand ... audiences will find these pages effortless, entertaining reading.'

—*Kirkus Reviews*

'By the end of the book, it's not as if you're saying goodbye to a writer, but a friend, a reliable companion ... puts forth some spellbinding research ... attempts to pulverise existing myths.'

—*The Pioneer*

'Like having a personal mentor ... both effective and genuine. Conversational, with a wonderful sense of honesty.'

—*Non-Fiction Authors Association Awards*

'A different thrill.'

—*The Hindu*

LEADERSHIP IN 100 WORDS

LEADERSHIP IN 100 WORDS

Simple Tips for Complex Challenges

Mainak Dhar

B L O O M S B U R Y

NEW DELHI • LONDON • OXFORD • NEW YORK • SYDNEY

BLOOMSBURY INDIA
Bloomsbury Publishing India Pvt. Ltd
Second Floor, LSC Building No. 4, DDA Complex, Pocket C – 6 & 7,
Vasant Kunj, New Delhi, 110070

BLOOMSBURY, BLOOMSBURY INDIA and the Diana logo
are trademarks of Bloomsbury Publishing Plc

First published in India 2022
This edition published 2022

ISBN: PB: 978-93-54355-50-9; eBook: 978-93-54355-51-6
2 4 6 8 10 9 7 5 3 1

Typeset in Fournier MT Std by Manipal Technologies Limited
Printed and bound in India by Thomson Press India Ltd.

FSC www.fsc.org
MIX
Paper from responsible sources
FSC® C010615

To find out more about our authors and books, visit www.bloomsbury.com and sign up for our newsletters

As always,
for Puja and Aaditya

'Sometimes the questions are complicated and the answers are simple.'

—*Dr Seuss*

CONTENTS

A Brief History of Mentoring

'Education is not the filling of a pot but the lighting of a fire.'

—W.B. Yeats

Today, the word 'mentor' conjures up images of someone in a corporate context, perhaps an older or more experienced leader, helping a younger colleague succeed by tapping into their experience.

The origin of the concept, and the word itself, however, has nothing to do with the corporate world. The history of mentoring goes back several millennia, and the word itself comes from the character Mentor in *The Odyssey* by Homer, written over 3,000 years ago. When the titular character, Odysseus, leaves home to participate in what comes to be known as the Trojan War, he entrusts his old friend Mentor to care for and teach his son, Telemachus. The goddess Athena takes the guise of Mentor and helps Telemachus grow from a diffident, underconfident and disconnected boy into a confident young man, who embarks on a perilous journey to find his father and engages in battles against numerous adversaries.

In today's corporate world, the new leader does not have to embark on journeys through dangerous waters or engage in combat with spear-wielding adversaries, but the broad philosophy of mentoring has changed remarkably little since those days. Once, when Telemachus is beset with doubt and wondering what to say, Mentor tells him, 'The words you will find within yourself.'

That is what makes for a great mentor, then and now. Someone who does not lay out all the answers but guides you to discover your own answers, find your own voice, become your own leader.

The genesis of this book—though at that time I had no idea there was a book involved somewhere down the line—lies in a mentoring conversation with someone in my team in the middle of 2019. We were chatting after work, and he was asking for feedback and advice related to his career. He had been newly promoted to a leadership role and was dealing with some thorny issues related to managing change and conflict in his team. I told him something and proceeded to finish the fresh lime soda that I was drinking. When I looked up, he was still looking at me, and then he said something I had not expected. He asked me a simple question.

'How did you make that so simple? You didn't tell me what to do, but by thinking about the questions you suggested I ask myself, it is clear what I need to do.'

That question took me by surprise. I had not thought consciously about it, but I responded to his question tapping not just into what my opinion was at that point in time, but by tapping into all the things I had learnt from working around and observing some truly amazing leaders, mentors and coaches in my career. The best of these mentors taught me that the best way to tackle complex challenges and questions was to try and simplify them down to what really mattered, and then to help people and teams focus on the few things that would make a difference. My best mentors had instilled in me, much like Mentor to Telemachus, that teaching people how to think about issues was always more powerful than telling them what to do.

Then my colleague asked me another question that stumped me.

'Why don't you write and share that advice with others?'

I had no idea why I would do that and why he would think that was important, but he told me that what I said made a lot of sense to him and got him to think of the issue he was facing in a very different way. When I came home, I thought of what he said and reflected on what had shaped my growth as a manager and a leader. Sure, I learnt some things in business school and also learnt many things in training and workshops. But I learnt a lot more through my own experiences in the corporate sector, both in my successes and failures. Perhaps, the richest learnings happened not in a classroom or boardroom but in spontaneous conversations with mentors and people I respected and learnt from. Simple things they said made me think of issues differently and made me relook my choices and clarified my mind on how to approach various issues. Importantly, they transmitted to me things that can never be transmitted in a classroom or through a slide deck in a corporate boardroom. Perhaps, the most important of those lessons had been the fact that leaders existed to serve their teams, and that success for a leader rested in that. As with Mentor and Telemachus, I realised that most often the best mentors I had learnt from did not just give me ready answers but helped me ask the right questions and ignited a spark in me that led me to discover the solutions that would work for me.

As I thought about it, I realised that those mentors were not just people whom I met in the corporate world. If anything, I learnt more about the core values of leadership from people who had nothing to do with the corporate world. My experience in the corporate world may have helped me put the words, frameworks and context to what they taught me, but I was lucky to have learnt from a very diverse group of mentors. They included, in no particular order, a freedom fighter who had spent time in jail, a spy, a karate sensei and a woman who overcame her terror of ice skating.

That evening I sat down with my laptop and began typing a post on LinkedIn. I have never been a fan of giving gratuitous advice and have never been one for much theory. So I wanted to write in as few words as possible what I had just told my colleague, while eschewing all theories and focusing on simple, straightforward and practical advice from my experience, and what I had learnt from my mentors. My first attempt led to a 103-word post. I finessed it down to 100 and, without much thought, added a hashtag.

#leadershipin100words

A year later, many things changed. We all went through the nightmare of COVID-19. Being cocooned at home, cut off from physical contact and with so many people facing career uncertainties, I began posting more regularly.

My posts sought to answer questions that came my way in many ways—questions that people asked me at work, which came up in mentoring conversations with young leaders I was mentoring, comments and questions in response to my earlier posts, and questions that were posed to me when I interacted with students during talks and guest lectures. My posts essentially sought to frame in 100 words my experiences, observations and learnings from great managers, bosses and mentors. All with the same hashtag. In a world where communication channels became increasingly restricted, this became a way for me to continue doing what I enjoy the most—writing and connecting with people through ideas. These posts sparked conversations, which led to more questions, which led to more posts.

At that time, I had already begun working on my book *Brand New Start*, which was sparked by mentoring conversations I had been having in the early days of the pandemic. It started off with a specific purpose. I put out an open offer on LinkedIn, offering to help people with career advice. Several people reached out, largely young managers in their early careers who did not have established mentors and networks. As I chatted with them—helping someone prepare for an interview, guiding another to brush up on their resume and discussing with yet another person which career option would be right for her—I realised that I was repeating myself on many themes, especially around having a clear sense of purpose versus chasing someone else's definition of success, being clear about one's differentiators versus just relying on degrees and designations, and showing up more thoughtfully at key 'moments of truth'. That led to *Brand New Start*, a book that aimed to help young managers develop a more authentic, more compelling and more differentiated personal brand to fast-start their careers.

A lot of the feedback, comments and questions I got on my #leadershipin100words posts reinforced what I felt while writing *Brand New Start*—that there were a lot of young leaders out there coming to grips with what it meant to lead a team without a mentor or a support system. That made writing the posts more enjoyable because each post was not just me putting something out there into cyberspace but a way for me to tangibly connect with people and, perhaps even in a small way, help them with their leadership questions.

Fast forward to another year or so, a friend asked me another question that led me to first think of taking these ideas beyond LinkedIn posts. The question was simple.

'You said your last post had some 15,000 views. You've been writing a lot of these. How many views do your posts have?'

I had no idea. How many views my posts had was hardly something I thought about or something that mattered to me. When I checked the last few posts and told my friend how many views they added up to, he whistled and asked me how many posts I had written. That was easier to check because they were all saved in a folder on my laptop. He did some quick mental math and then asked another question.

'You probably have a million or more views. That is a lot of people you're reaching with these.'

The number meant nothing to me, except that I was connecting with many more people and much more deeply than I may have thought possible when I started typing my first post. More recently, a couple of people asked me in the comments to my posts why I did not put together in a book form all the thoughts I had been sharing.

I thought of why I had written *Brand New Start*. I thought of how fulfilling it had been to connect with people and to try and impact them positively in any small way I could. I thought of all the questions and comments my #leadershipin100words posts had got and all the new connections and relationships I had formed through them. I thought of the many new leaders out there who wished they had a mentor but did not. An article on July 2019 in *Forbes* by Christina Comaford cited that 76 per cent of people think mentors are important but only 37 per cent have one. There were many young leaders out there who could do with a little helpful nudge from a mentor.

I realised my friend was right.

That's how this book was born.

This book is, therefore, the outcome of a series of questions that made me rethink how I could apply some of the things I most enjoy about being a business leader and a mentor, with the privilege and opportunity to help others grow. Equally, it brings to life what I enjoy the most about being a writer—the opportunity to positively impact and connect with people through my words and ideas.

As I began writing this book, I realised it was also an opportunity for me to pay forward all I have learnt from my mentors and coaches over the years about how one can be a stronger leader and share those lessons with others. What you hold in your hands is, therefore, not just a compilation of my personal learnings and opinions but the values, insights and principles I have picked up over my 25-year career in the corporate sector, working for, around and being mentored by some amazing leaders. Leaders like Chip Bergh, Ravi Chaturvedi, Shantanu Khosla, Sonny Iqbal, Jim Lafferty, Christina Law, Joanne Crewes, Nayantara Bali, Vivek Bali, Sam Kim, Jerson Uy and Aaron Powell.

Perhaps even more so, this book is a tribute to the personal mentors who shaped me into the person I became and instilled in me the core values that made me intuitively appreciate what good leadership looked like from a young age. I was blessed to have great role models to learn from, like Satyen De Chowdhury, my maternal grandfather, who spent time in jail during India's freedom struggle and then joined the police force of a newly independent India; my father, Maloy Krishna Dhar, who carved a storied career for himself as an intelligence officer and then reinvented himself as a bestselling author; and last but by no means least, my mother, Sunanda Dhar, who taught me that the most powerful thing you can do to help someone overcome their fear of change and the unknown is by holding their hand and embracing that change with them.

In a way, this book is my tribute to them for having helped me appreciate the joy of helping others grow and just how much can be learnt through the simple act of engaging in meaningful mentoring conversations and helping others find simple, straightforward ways to think of addressing complex questions.

Imagine that you are not just holding a book in your hands, but that this is an opportunity to engage in a mentoring conversation with me on leadership—for me to channel my experiences and the wisdom of the many amazing mentors I have been blessed to have and to help you think about common leadership challenges you may be facing. This book is not a destination, an ending point, where you get all the answers, certainly not a repository of all the 'right' answers, but a provocation, a catalyst, to spark your thoughts about how you might approach common leadership challenges and dilemmas. As you read this book, do not focus only on the answers but also on the questions themselves. Leadership is not something to which there are magical 'right' answers. I have provided some perspective given my experiences and learnings, but maybe something else works for you. What is important, sometimes, is not necessarily having a ready 'right' answer, but in asking the right questions and then having an open mind in seeking alternative ways of thinking about them. Just as Mentor inspires Telemachus, my intention is not to feed you answers but often to light the spark that will enable you to come up with answers that will work uniquely for you.

Here are a few different ways you could use this book.

If you already have a specific question or area of concern on your mind, I have split this book into three sections based on common challenges leaders face—leading others, leading through change and leading yourself. Just go to the section you think will be most helpful in answering the question you have in mind and dive right in.

If you do not have a specific question in mind but would just want to learn more about some of the common leadership questions I have tried to answer, then, of course, read it through and see which section or portions resonate with you.

Leadership is an applied skill, not something you will get better at just by reading a book and musing over what you have learnt by yourself. As you spot a question that resonates with you or an answer that you think could be of use in resolving a challenge you are facing, try and apply it. See what works and what does not in your real-world leadership challenges and reflect on it through a process of continuous learning. At the end of each section, I have provided space for you to reflect on these and to capture any additional questions you might have.

Ready to start our conversation?

Great! Let us start tackling some common leadership challenges with simple bite-sized advice.

One hundred words at a time.

Leading Others

> 'A leader is best when people barely know he exists, when his work is done, his aim fulfilled, they will say: we did it ourselves.'
>
> —Lao Tzu

The first 'team' I led consisted of a plastic rat and two balloons shaped like koalas. I was an assistant brand manager early in my career. I was young and this was my way of both fooling around a bit at work and poking a bit of irreverent fun at what I saw some leaders around me doing, which was delegating everything downwards. So when someone would ask me how I was progressing on some work I had been given, I would point to the rat or the koalas and give them feedback on how they needed to be more proactive in updating me on their progress on the responsibilities I had assigned to them.

A little bit later, I got real people as direct reports for the first time in my career, and I soon realised that it was a very different ball game. For one, human beings have feelings, and as a young leader, I realised that I was responsible in many ways for shaping how my team felt. That realisation first struck home to me when our team, which was working on a business that was in a fair bit of trouble, was not given a chance to present before a senior global leader, as they ran out of time, and we were not a priority. I walked out of the room and saw my three team members standing there, their shoulders slumped, eyes downcast. As I took them out for lunch and worked on getting their spirits up, I realised just how much of what I said and did affected them personally.

As I grew in my career, I came to realise the responsibilities that came with being a leader. You are responsible for not just shaping someone else's career but impacting their lives and that of their families in a very tangible way. At the same time, I learnt to embrace the joy of being a leader, the joy of knowing that you could, through what you do and say, make a positive impact on someone. You could help someone grow, learn, adapt and succeed. The biggest joys in my 25-year-long career weren't when I achieved some brilliant business results but when I helped, even if in a small way, someone succeed beyond their expectations.

I have learnt a lot about leading teams from many people. I have worked for and around some great leaders in my career, and watching them in action has been a great source of learning. I have, of course, learnt from my own experiences, successes and failures alike. However, as I realised what it meant to lead people, I realised there was a lot I could tap into from a source that had nothing to do with MBA classes in business schools, HR training in boardrooms or advice from bosses at workplaces. These learnings came from a lifetime of conversations and observations revolving around my grandfather and father. Both served in the police, and so a life spent growing up around men in uniform, who routinely put their lives on the line for each other, taught me a lot about what it took to lead men. Sitting on the terrace of my grandfather's house in Kolkata, drinking beer with him to celebrate his 80th birthday, I remember telling him how I was about to begin my corporate career in a couple of months. He began by telling me that success in any field is rarely about how smart you are. I'd realise it one day, he said, that it all boils down to one thing.

Could you get your people to follow you not because of your rank but because of how you treated them?

My maternal grandfather was an interesting man. As a young adult in the heady days of the freedom struggle, he spent time in jail for resisting British rule. Despite being a brilliant student, he refused to entertain the idea of taking a job in the colonial government. When India gained Independence in 1947, he was among independent India's first batch of Indian Police Service (IPS) officers. He told me stories about leading from the front, of never asking his men to take risks he would not take himself and of how the men put everything on the line, not for the paycheck or the next promotion but for the man next to him. That was the sense of camaraderie, loyalty and pride that kept him and his men going. My father, who himself spent a long career in the police and then in the shadowy world of intelligence, would tell me about what made a person put his life on the line—not for the money but for a purpose and a cause greater than him. A great leader was ultimately someone who would define such a cause, live up to it and have their people's back when the rubber hits the road. I've seen my father return from missions in which he'd put himself at great personal risk, which someone at his level could have avoided. He'd rather risk himself than abandon his men.

My father and grandfather are no more, but I have often found myself tapping into their wisdom whenever I am in a leadership dilemma. More often than not, the simplicity and straight talk of men in uniform have stood me well and shaped me as a person and a leader in many ways. As I reflect on my life, they were perhaps the best coaches on leadership I have ever had, though at that time I wasn't aware of this profound insight.

Not surprisingly, a large number of questions I have been asked on leadership, especially from young leaders early in their journey of leading teams, has been on how they can motivate, grow and lead their people. Here are some of them, along with my straight answers.

One hundred words at a time.

I have seen leaders who seem obsessed with their success, and all that matters is their promotion, bonus or growth. It feels like their people and team members are just resources to be used to help them succeed. As I grow to be a leader myself, how do I balance my success with the success of my team or the people who are working for me?

When a leader's starting point is 'what's in it for me?', that leader has lost a lot of credibility and legitimacy. Some people obsess about their personal success or promotions without focusing on what success means for those who depend on them or work for them. Real leaders are not guided by personal success, but they regard it as a natural outcome of helping their people succeed. Focus your energies on how your team can succeed, and often you will find your success follow suit. Focusing on oneself will demotivate the team, which will often lead to failure for everyone.

As a new leader, I feel under pressure from my team to get results. At the same time, I am told I need to engage with them. How do I balance the two? Also, I am an employee myself. Who thinks of engaging with or motivating me? Where do I find the energy to both inspire my people and get inspired myself?

'What have you done for me lately?' asked the manager. 'When was the last time I felt inspired?' asked the employee. Memo to bosses—stop flogging your people for results; ask what difference you are making to them. People are at their best when they feel valued and part of something bigger than themselves. Memo to employees—don't wait for inspiration from your boss but seek it in who you can make a positive difference to through your colleagues, consumers, community or, indeed, your own employees. The best way to feel inspired is to pay it forward by inspiring someone.

I have recently been promoted into a leadership role. How do I get my people to see me as a leader? My former boss used to tell me that what matters is where you are in the hierarchy of the organisation. I am not so sure that is how it works anymore, especially with younger employees. Any advice on what I could do to get my people to see me as their leader?

There is a difference between being a leader and having followers. You can be appointed to a leadership position. Your business card can carry the title. You can have the fancy office that proclaims your status. All that and yet nobody may follow you. They may obey you but never really follow you. Leadership that creates followers is earned and not appointed. It doesn't matter what your business card says or whether you have a fancy office or a plebeian cubicle. What matters is that you are seen to exist to help your people shine. Not the other way around.

I just offered a young employee a great opportunity, but she turned it down saying it did not fit with what her priorities were. I was stunned. When I was her age, I would have grabbed such a career opportunity if it came my way! As a leader, how can I better understand what my people want or define as success?

A reminder for leaders: Don't assume that what motivates you also motivates your team. A leader about to retire may look at stock prices, bonuses and legacy, but the youngest member of the team, who has a long career ahead, will look for inspiration, learning and growth. Spend time with the 'troops' outside of reviews and meetings. Use your experience to not just judge but teach. Learn what motivates your people and what help they need to achieve success as they define it. Most of all, remember you, too, were young, hungry and idealistic once, so inspire by tapping into that empathy.

I just got promoted to a leadership position and I can already feel the weight of responsibility. My former boss told me that the biggest difference I can feel is that now the buck stops with me. I am accountable for the whole P&L, across all lines, and I need to rise above being a functional leader and be a true business leader. I get that and it makes sense. Any other advice as I settle into my new leadership role?

Some leaders take pride in managing P&L well. That's fine as long as they don't lose sight of the most important 'P'—people. If a leader gets the right people on their team; inspires them with a compelling vision; helps them learn, grow and succeed; profits and business results always follow. In the absence of that, the pursuit of profits without taking people along may lead to results, but only in the short term. True leaders understand that their legacy is not just the P&L they leave behind but also the leaders they've helped to lead the business after them.

1 MILLION+ LINKEDIN VIEWS

Times are tough in our industry and for our businesses. My bosses keep putting pressure on me to deliver and I need to get my team to deliver as well. A couple of my team members have quit already, and I don't know how to balance between the need to deliver on our commitments and not putting so much pressure on people that they'll want to leave their jobs. What could I do differently?

When times are tough, many leaders focus on short-term deliveries. That is appropriate because there will be no bright future if you do not fix the now. The answer is in balance. A phrase I have heard many times is 'if the house is burning, you focus on putting out the fire'. True, but balance that by asking what happens when the fire is out. People's motivation to put out the fire (versus running away) will depend on either the fear of being homeless or the prospect of a nicer house. Hope is always a more powerful motivator than fear.

I have been appointed in my new leadership role. My bosses tell me things like I need to think of the legacy I want to leave behind as a leader. What does that even mean? How can I think of that in a way that is simple to understand? Will it only depend on the performance of the business I'd have left behind when I am finished with this role?

Most people make New Year's resolutions that focus on themselves (lose weight). Businesses also make such self-centred 'resolutions' (grow profits and margins). As a leader, try and do things differently. Make resolutions for others—help someone land on their feet, give someone advice when they need it most, help someone become more successful than they may have imagined possible. People won't remember the profits you delivered in a particular quarter, but they will remember the difference you made to them long after you're gone. Define your legacy not by business results but by the positive impact you leave on people.

All the HR training sessions I go to teach me that as a leader I need to motivate and inspire my people. How do I do that? Some of my colleagues say that it boils down to helping people get a promotion, earn good bonuses and move ahead in their careers. Is it as simple as that? Are there any other strategies I could use to motivate my people?

Different leaders have different views on what motivates people. Some believe in inspirational goals while others in learning and growth. There are still others who think of bonuses, increments and career progression. All of which are valid and important, but many leaders overlook that ultimately, they work for people around them. You build empathy and trust, and get to value people as human beings, not as resources or boxes in an organisational chart. These enable people to follow you, not just for the journey ahead but for who you are. Rewards buy short-term compliance; trust and empathy earn long-term commitment.

1 MILLION+ LINKEDIN VIEWS

I have moved into a new leadership role and my boss expects me to make an early impact. How do I best do that? Should I try and find some areas where I can make quick and visible changes? I have a bunch of ideas that came to me during the onboarding process. How soon do I share those with my new team, or do I wait a bit longer until I've settled in? How soon is a new leader expected to have the answers anyway?

Beware of leaders, especially new ones, who pretend to have all the answers. Often these answers are nothing more than a reflection of their own biases and experiences and may not have the team's buy-in or even be suitable or executable, given their contexts and capabilities. The best leaders do not rush to give answers or pretend to have all the answers. They focus on asking the right questions and then getting the people and capabilities in place to help find the answers. Such an approach leads to a greater team buy-in and the chances of being executed with excellence.

My former boss used to often say that we should be 'entrepreneurial'. He never did tell us exactly what that meant and always worked in a very 'old school' and hierarchical way. However, now that I am in a leadership role myself, I find that so many of my younger colleagues want more empowerment and would love to work in a less bureaucratic setup. Any thoughts on how I could create such an environment for them? Also, how do I not make the same mistakes my former boss made?

Many leaders in large companies talk of behaving like a start-up. They think this means being more accessible, less rigid and more risk-taking. All good steps, but often they miss out on two elements. They continue to have a sense of entitlement that comes with being a cog in the wheel of a large company (My budget should be Y because it was X last year), and they focus more on and get lost in the maze of internal structures, politics and bureaucracy (This region or that function did this), as opposed to being obsessed with winning consumers and customers.

My boss just told me that I have been promoted to the role of a team leader. I am really excited as it is a big move for me. He tells me how I will now have an office cabin of my own and how he had felt when he got his first cabin as a leader. What do you make of those who say that open offices are better versus those who feel that leaders should have visible symbols, such as a cabin or an office?

Some managers speak of aspiring for the corner office. Office furniture does not make you a leader, serving your team and helping them succeed does. I've never had an office or a cabin, and it works for me. However, I understand if others want one. What matters is that leaders spend most of their time with their teams—in stores, factories, with consumers and customers—serving where help is most needed, not behind the desk. Whether you aspire for a cabin or not, focus on the size of your impact on those you serve, not the size of your office.

Some of my peers kept talking about how taking on larger teams and bigger budgets was one way to think of making a big impact. I have read some of your articles where you've said that the core impact that leaders make is on their people. How could I build myself to be able to make a bigger impact on my team?

Weak leaders focus on the size of their 'empire'; strong leaders ask whom they serve. It's easier said than done because you will not learn this in business schools or from most bosses. Drawing from personal experience, one way to build a service mindset is to get involved in service outside of one's work—volunteer for a cause you are passionate about, teach kids, mentor young people in their careers. These will teach you empathy and the joy of helping others without expecting anything in return, useful skills for a leader but not taught in MBA classes or most boardrooms.

I have just stepped into a leadership role, and part of my orientation is understanding the span of control of my role. So I am spending time with my HR colleagues, learning the organisational chart and understanding reporting lines. I am also working with my finance colleagues to understand where I have approval rights and where my role fits in the decision-making process. When I asked why they were so fixated on this, I've been told that my predecessor was very focused on what he could or couldn't control. I think it is a bit of an overkill to obsess over it instead of getting on with the work to be done and the team I am supposed to lead. Am I on the right track?

Some managers get fixated on what they control (people, budgets, decisions) when they evaluate leadership roles in an organisation. Here is a reality—true leaders control nothing. The only ones who control our business are employees who choose to work for us, consumers who choose to buy our brands and partners who choose to support us. Do right for them, serve them, understand them and meet their needs, and you and your business will thrive. Next time someone talks about a leadership role, don't obsess about the span of control but understand the span of service—who do you serve?

I am in a leadership role. There is a young employee in my team who seems to revel in being different. He wears more casual clothes than others and is often seen listening to music on his AirPods, both of which reflect an air of not being serious at the workplace. My boss says he is not a good fit for our team as we want people who 'fit in'. The thing is, he is good at what he does and delivers, and he does not rub anyone the wrong way. I can understand him, though. Young people are different from, say, my boss' generation. What do you feel about this—leading employees from a very different generation?

Weak leaders rush to judge employees based on the 'how' (style, personality). Most leaders focus on the 'what' (results, milestones). Great leaders also insist on the 'why' (motivations, fit, capability), which can often mean the difference between helping someone to succeed versus judging them too hastily. Great leaders know that their role is not of an examiner but that of a coach. They understand the unique personalities, strengths and motivations of their people and how best they can be helped to succeed, instead of assuming that every employee must be a carbon copy of each other or the leader.

1 MILLION+ LINKEDIN VIEWS

I am going to be presenting before my new team a direction we want to take. I have got a bunch of slides with lots of data and the rationale behind the new direction. My boss made me modify the slides several times, and I think I am finally ready. I am new in the role; my predecessor was around for a long time and was much loved by the team. In addition to the strategies and slides, any other advice on how I could get off on the right foot with my new team?

What inspires teams to the next level? Data? Strategies? Direction? All of them, plus one more ingredient. Most big decisions we make in life are driven not just by facts but also by emotion. The best leaders inspire not through data and strategies but by winning hearts and minds—a compelling purpose, an inspiring mission, a personal touch, trust and empathy. So when you try and rally a team to pursue big goals or deal with adversity, remember they are looking not only at your slides but also your body language, your tone of voice and the emotion you transmit.

I am a new team leader and we just failed on a project. We were all very emotionally invested in this project and the failure has come as a big blow. My team is demoralised and I want to get them back on their feet. Anything I can do to help them bounce back and stay motivated?

None of us can always be successful, but we can always be authentic and have a learning mindset. When you fail as a leader, share what you have learnt with your team and how it taught you things that will help you be more successful in the future. Take accountability for your decisions that may have led to the failure instead of blaming others. Talk about how in the past you bounced back from failure. All these will help shape you as a role model for your team and encourage them to confront failure, learn from it and emerge stronger.

I am new in a leadership role and I am trying to strengthen my team. I have a few people on my team who know the business well and have worked with me before, so we know each other well and are on the same wavelength. Now my boss wants me to fill the team with more folks who have worked on our teams before—people with a similar way of thinking—as he feels it will make the team function more smoothly. I worry about that because our industry is going through a lot of changes and we need fresh ideas. How should a new leader think of a way to balance between known faces and fresh talent?

Insecure leaders want to surround themselves with people who agree with them and reinforce their worldview. Secure leaders know that the best thing to do is to have diverse voices around them, including those who will stretch their minds and bring fresh ideas and voices to the table. The best teams—the ones that can adapt, evolve and shape the future—are formed by leaders who do not enforce consensus, comfort and conformity but encourage an environment where people can feel they will be heard, where diversity of thoughts is encouraged and viewed as essential for progress and growth.

Here is an important but pretty mundane dilemma I am facing as a new leader. My predecessor seemingly used to have his calendar filled from morning to evening with meetings. His team, now mine, consistently gave unflattering feedback in surveys, saying how these meetings suck up so much time and energy, especially in preparation for each meeting. Are such meetings an inevitable part of leadership roles?

Some leaders turn meetings into big jamborees, with innumerable hours of slides and huge crowds in the room or on call. Teams spend hours preparing for these, while secretly wishing for a clearer direction and more time to do the real work. We should all try not to be such leaders. Call meetings only when needed, and try and achieve what is required in the least possible time with the least paperwork involved by focusing only on what is critical. Success is getting the job done and helping your people succeed, not in the number of meetings, calls or slides.

I am hiring for a really important role in my team, one in which the selected person will lead some critical projects and hopefully succeed me one day. So I need to hire someone who is not just capable of doing the job today but can also grow with our organisation in the long term. Any tips on how I could approach such an interview?

I've learnt a lesson after conducting many interviews to hire people—do not judge a candidate just by their answers but pay close attention to the questions they ask. Most candidates come prepared with what they think will be the right answers, but only a few candidates display the curiosity to ask insightful questions about the organisation, beyond the role on offer or its function. Rather than focusing only on work to be done, this lot also exhibit self-awareness to ask questions on the organisational culture, their likely fit in it and the perceptiveness to ask how work gets done.

We have reviews coming up with the CEO. My team and I have been spending a lot of time getting all our materials ready. A couple of other leaders I know are using this time to rehearse, to ensure they have all the answers and to make changes to their slides. My team is young and many of them are nervous about presenting for the first time before the CEO, and as their leader, I want to make sure we all show up well. Any tips on how to pull off a successful meeting with a senior leader?

Some leaders make their people spend hours 'rehearsing' for big meetings with senior leaders, orchestrating who says what, re-editing slides and trying to appear 'buttoned down'. Good leaders know the best meetings with senior leaders are not about putting up a performance but having a dialogue; not to pretend to have all the answers but to raise tough questions, to share progress and to be genuinely open to ideas and builds; not to focus on re-editing slides but to realise that the focus should be on people and ideas. Slides should be an aid, not the focus of the meeting.

With the pandemic and the many changes it has brought along, we have been working remotely for a long time. I am fine with it but some of my peers complain that they do not like working remotely as it keeps them apart. They want their team members around them to ensure everyone is working on agreed priorities. Given that some sort of remote working is likely to be a fact of life for us, at least for a few days a week, do you have any view on this?

Over the last few challenging months, leaders have had to adapt to working remotely and many have thrived. However, a few struggled, claiming they need people in front of them, that they can't be sure if people are working at home. Being together does develop camaraderie and collaboration, but great leaders create an impact that does not always need physical proximity. It stems from a clarity of purpose and direction, empathy, trust, being accessible and being able to adapt to change and challenges. Leaders complaining about remote working need to realise the issue is not about 'remote' but their leadership agility.

As a woman leader, I cringe sometimes when my bosses say they want 'to encourage diversity'. I mean, does that not reflect a patronising attitude? What is your point of view on how some leaders take such a view on diversity?

When leaders say they want to 'encourage more diversity' or 'give an opportunity to diverse talent', they are totally missing the point. Leaders who have poor diversity in their teams are not doing anybody any favour by building stronger diversity. They are making up for a failure of their leadership in not having a more representative team that includes diversity in all its dimensions to drive better decisions and outcomes. Building diversity, especially at senior levels, can take time, but a good starting point is one of intent and mindset—acting with urgency and taking stronger personal accountability for its shortfall.

I am hiring for a couple of key roles. I have got a comprehensive checklist of the technical competencies, skills and experiences that I should look for. Here is my dilemma. I have two resumes in front of me, and they seem equal on all the above counts. What else could I look for?

Mark Murphy, bestselling author of *Hiring for Attitude*, tracked 20,000 new hires and found that 46 per cent of them failed in the first 18 months. Only 11 per cent failed due to lack of skills; 89 per cent failed due to attitudinal issues like low levels of emotional intelligence, motivation and temperament. In evaluating candidates, don't just check for skills and experiences but also look for fit and commitment. Try and understand their purpose—why they do what they do. Understand their fit with your organisational culture and whether their longer-term aspirations and motivations fit with what you offer.

It is that time of year (Christmas and New Year) once again, and, of course, we are thinking of gifts for our team members. Also, this is a time when we all make resolutions. As a new leader, I want to know how I can be a better leader. Any tips?

A great gift you can give anyone (an employee at work or your child at home) is the space to express their authentic self and be themselves. Sometimes, without realising it, bosses and parents seek to mould in their image those who look to them for direction and to impose on them their styles and biases, and their definitions of success. Lasting success and fulfilment usually come when we can be authentic, express who we are and play to our unique strengths. The best part is that this is a gift you can give every day without waiting for Christmas.

When I began working, my bosses were very particular about being 'professional'. They insisted on dressing in a certain way and keeping our personal lives out of the workplace. Now that I am a leader myself, how should I think of it, especially in the world of remote and hybrid workplaces?

Some believe that being 'professional' means focusing on work and hiding our 'personal side'. If anything, authentic leadership is about embracing one's full self and not be apologetic about it. In 2020, 'work' and 'personal' spaces became blurred, and 'office' was sometimes an old desk with kids' homework on it. We saw each other's homes instead of being in uniform cubicles, and we juggled calls while managing kids. The year was forgettable, but some lessons are worth remembering—we embraced our full selves, and began valuing and accepting our colleagues as people rather than as roles they play at work.

My team needs to come up with some innovative ideas. Doing what we have done before won't get us the results we want. The more I try to think differently or innovatively, the more I struggle to get away from the realities of the business world. As a leader, how can I inspire myself and my team to think out of the box?

Leaders often say they want out-of-the-box thinking. The best way to think out of the box is to take yourself out of the box. Here's how you may proceed. Cultivate diverse passions and hobbies that have nothing to do with your job; hang out with people with very different backgrounds, interests and perspectives than your own; allow yourself to re-energise when you unplug from work. Conversely, if leaders want out-of-the-box thinkers, they need to be comfortable with people who don't conform to their preconceived notions of 'fit', and they need to stop saying 'that's how things are done around here'.

I have worked with bosses who are experts in their fields, always knowing more than the rest of the team. Now I myself am in a leadership role, working in an industry I am not familiar with. I am hardly the subject matter expert, but I need to build a team to help us succeed. How can I approach it differently than, perhaps, my previous bosses?

Poor leaders want to be the ones with all the answers; they want to get people on their teams to do their biddings. Average leaders get people to reinforce their worldview; they look for people with similar experiences and skills as theirs. The best leaders are not afraid of being surrounded by people who might even have contrarian thoughts and experiences. Being a great leader is not about having all the answers; it is about being smart and humble enough to acknowledge what one does not know and to get others on the team to help fill in those gaps.

I like being around people, getting to know them and forming meaningful relationships. As I become a team leader, does it need to change? I have seen bosses who try and stay aloof and do not want to get too close to their people. That is not my natural style. Will it come in the way as I take on a new leadership role?

Some leaders think displaying empathy means 'being soft' and does not help performance. Perhaps, in the short term or when the going is good, focusing only on targets and incentives will work. However, in the long term, especially in times of uncertainty, it is critical that employees know their leaders care about them, that the employees are supported and their leaders have the employees' back. That makes teams stretch beyond the norm, support one another and take ownership. Empathy is basically about being a decent human being, but it can also be a powerful force multiplier in unlocking team performance.

1 MILLION+ LINKEDIN VIEWS

What is one simple everyday thing I could do to keep my team motivated and charged up? Something that does not require complicated checklists, models or concepts.

To be great at anything, you need to build muscle memory—repeatedly exercising certain skills, so that when needed, one can use them without conscious thought. One muscle memory that more leaders must build is to show appreciation. Not occasional performance appraisals, ratings or promotions but everyday acts of appreciation and gratitude. Saying thank you more often; making efforts to find things to appreciate versus criticise; looking at the glass half-full versus half-empty; smiling more often. They have always been important, but now more than ever, when all of us could do with feeling positive, valued and supported.

I have been told that part of being a strong leader is to inspire my team with a vision. I have seen some old bosses make big presentations to the team, but then outside of those it was very much business as usual, and I became a bit cynical about such leaders. How should I think about genuinely having a mission for my team and then following through on it?

Brands are not built through impressive PowerPoint decks or grand mission statements but by what they do to serve consumers. It's the same with building credible leadership. You impact the minds and hearts of others not by what you say but by what you do. Some leaders say they are open-minded but resist new ideas or say they are focused on people but watch out only for themselves. The best leaders are often those who do not spend much time making grand proclamations but get on with serving those counting on them and letting their actions do the speaking.

As a new leader, one of the things I find challenging is how to choose people for my team. Whether it is hiring from outside or evaluating internal candidates, I get conflicting advice. The 'official' job description that HR focuses on are qualifications and 'boxes' that need to be ticked in terms of past experiences. The problem is that I need some significant change to be made in my team in terms of how we work, and I need someone who can really challenge the status quo. How should I think of talent in such a context?

As leaders, at times we need to bet on people. Don't back people just because they are the conventional choice, and don't tick the 'boxes' in haste. If you get the opportunity, bet on people who are humble and hungry. Humble enough to know they do not know everything and are open to learning, and hungry enough to embrace change and challenge the status quo. Safe choices may do well in rowing the boat in the direction it is on, but sometimes the humble and hungry bets are what you need to row into uncharted waters or reimagine your destination.

1 MILLION+ LINKEDIN VIEWS

I have taken on a new role, and it is my first senior leadership position where I have a reasonably large team reporting to me. My predecessor believed in keeping a distance from the team. For example, he did not interact much with them outside of work, other than very formal events, and while he would share a lot of his experiences and learnings from previous roles, he was very guarded about sharing anything about his life outside of work. He told me that he felt his team needed to respect him and that a leader in a role like this should show up professionally. To be honest, that did not work for me, as I have always felt that it is better to let my teammates know who I am and what makes me tick. Does that change when I become a senior leader?

Some leaders conform to a stereotype of how someone in their role 'should show up'; they do not reveal much of their individuality to their teams beyond the work at hand. I feel that can restrict your impact. Share what values you grew up with, what is important to you beyond work, what you are passionate about, how you spend your free time. Being task-oriented may help deliver short-term results but being authentic helps you build true commitment and encourages others around you to bring their full, authentic selves and diverse thinking to work. That's critical in creating lasting success.

There are a couple of people in my team who seem to have very different ideas about how to approach issues. Often, this boils over into heated debates. Both are very experienced managers and are very good at what they do. The rest of my team is generally very collaborative and operates with a high degree of consensus. Should I be worried about having two of my experienced team members often disagreeing with each other?

Conflict by itself is neither good nor bad. What is important is the reason behind the conflict. If it is because there are team members with divergent views or experiences and are trying to provide solutions with the best interests of the team in mind, then channelise the conflict by harnessing diverse viewpoints and ideas. Constructive challenges and conflict can often lead to better outcomes than everyone agreeing on everything. However, if the conflict is because of ego, politics or turf issues, then you need to step in and lay down expectations on how you want the team to operate.

I am a new leader in my team. One of my direct reports is a veteran sales manager, who is widely acknowledged as an expert in what he does. He has a lot more experience than me, and there is a lot to learn from him. My predecessor used to think of him as someone who could rise even higher in the organisation, but as I interact more with him, I realise he has some issues. He has very archaic views on women in the workforce, and sometimes comes across as extremely sexist. That is not the tone I would like my senior leaders to set, which is also not in line with the culture of our organisation. How should I reconcile his excellence at his job with his ignominious side?

Corporate leaders often talk about the importance of driving inclusion and diversity. Here is a simpler take on it. Being inclusive and not excluding or demeaning people on the basis of gender or sexual orientation or background has less to do with meeting any corporate norms and more to do with just being fit to be part of any progressive organisational future. No matter how great someone may be at their work, being dismissive of others because of their gender or sexual orientation not only shows a lack of sensitivity but shows that they are likely unfit for broader leadership roles.

My organisation strongly believes in doing business ethically, and that is part of the reason I have enjoyed building my career here. However, as with all large organisations, some leaders interpret this differently. I have recently moved into a new leadership role where I discovered that one of my direct reports is always looking to cut corners by taking advantage of ambiguity. He says he is doing it for the good of the business and my predecessor seemed to have been ignoring this behaviour. I am uncomfortable because it sends a wrong signal to other employees. What kind of role model will this person be if he ever becomes a senior leader in our team? My predecessor, who had rated him highly, thought he could be promoted to more senior roles. I am confused, please comment.

Gichin Funakoshi, the founder of modern karate, said 'spirit first, technique second'. This also applies to the corporate world. When evaluating people, some leaders focus overly on technique (skills, competence and short-term results) but not enough on the spirit (values, motivation and culture fit). A technique is necessary but not sufficient for long-term success. Those with strong technique but 'weak spirit' (poor fit with organisational culture, values and ethics) will often have limited potential. In the corporate world, as in karate, the technique is usually teachable; the spirit is often what differentiates a reliable, solid performer from someone who can be a future leader.

With the COVID-19 pandemic and all the changes and uncertainty it brought for all of us, I often think about what I can do as a leader to show my team members that they are cared for and supported. We do town halls, have adapted our policies to be more supportive, and try and have a lot of communication with them. Is there anything else I could do personally as a leader?

Before my first Zoom presentation to our CEO in my new job, my son quietly placed his favourite stuffed toy, George, beside me so I would be confident as George would take all the tough questions. Unknown to those I was presenting to, George sat next to me, and I smiled thinking of my son. As leaders, to support our people and show them we care for them, we don't need big policies, grand pronouncements or posters on office walls. What often matters most are, as my son taught me, small random acts of kindness and empathy.

We are living through times where we need to be resilient. That puts a lot of added pressure on a leader because you now not only have to be resilient but also show up as being resilient before your team. Any thoughts on how to be resilient?

I rediscovered an old email from my father, written over 20 years ago, when I was upset about a setback. His last line was 'Move on, grow, learn, understand what to do differently next time. Being hurt is okay, sometimes it makes you tougher.' He passed away in 2012, but reading the mail a couple of months ago, I felt like he was reaching out to me with advice for times when we need to be resilient as people and leaders. Resilience is not about being unaffected by setbacks but about learning from them—letting go of negativity and emerging stronger, self-aware and positive.

Some old-school leaders still seem to think that it's important how long an employee stays in office, and tend to view such employees as harder working or more committed. What's your view on that?

Why do some leaders judge employees' commitment and contribution by the long hours they put in? Why do they focus on the appearance of effort and hours clocked as against outcomes delivered? While we all need to stretch at times, shouldn't an employee who can deliver outstanding results without habitually working late actually be appreciated for being more efficient, better at planning or just more capable? The same leaders often focus on how to run their businesses with maximum efficiency. If they apply the same mindset to their organisations' time and energy, would they think differently about how they lead and assess people?

Some leaders I have worked with seem to believe that leaders must be aggressive and pushy, and that being 'tough' is an important aspect of being a strong leader. I am personally introverted by nature, so that does not always resonate with me. What's your advice on this?

Why do some leaders think being aggressive or pushy are signs of being a go-getter or results-oriented? The toughest people I've met, from intelligence and military officers to karate masters, have been unassuming and humble. What makes them tough is that they are deeply purpose-driven, take setbacks in their stride, seek to improve, are confident in their abilities and, when needed, concentrate those into focused action to get jobs done. In your teams, don't just focus on the loudest or those who itch to showcase themselves. Often your stars will be the quiet ones with true inner toughness.

Reflection Sheet on Leading Others

What am I going to apply at my workplace and with my team?

How do these questions and answers spark my mind to think differently about leading?

What additional questions do I have that are not covered here?

Leading through Change

'Yesterday I was clever, so I wanted to change the world. Today I am wise, so I am changing myself.'

—Jalaluddin Rumi

Dealing with change is something I was very used to long before I began my corporate career. Since my father's job was transferable, we moved around a lot when I was a kid, and I went through nine schools before I finished my education. Long before I heard about the importance of diversity and inclusion in corporate boardrooms, I learnt first-hand about what they meant. I was the first Indian kid in my class in Canada in the early 1980s, and a few years later, when we returned to India, I was the kid from abroad with a funny accent. My mother, who saw me deal with all these changes, told me something that I recall whenever I hear anyone talking about inclusion.

'Always reach out and welcome someone new because you know how wonderful it feels to be welcomed by strangers and how bad it is to be excluded or judged even before people get a chance to know you.'

She also taught me how to help lead others through change—not through lectures, charts or slides but her actions. In Canada, the lakes would freeze over in winter and a lot of my friends would go ice skating. I had never done it before and was terrified at the prospect. My mother knew I was missing out on the fun but understood how I was struggling to adapt to something completely alien to me. So she went ahead and got us a pair of ice skates each and then chaperoned me onto the ice rink by holding my hand. We fell numerous times, but it didn't matter because we fell together. I never thought of it back then (I was only 10 years old), but looking back now I marvel at her courage to do this in public for me. Soon I mustered up enough courage to venture out on the rink on my own. Perhaps, I realised that it was not the fear of ice skating per se that held me back but the fear of embarrassment from falling. My mother helped me get over that fear by demonstrating that it was okay to fail, that there was no embarrassment in it and that she was willing to be there by my side, falling with me. That was a powerful lesson I remember till this day.

Her words and actions have guided me throughout my life and career. As a result, being resilient has come naturally to me.

That was until I learnt what it meant to guide others through change.

The first time I encountered corporate restructuring was when I was barely three years into my career. I remember sitting in a large room listening to people discussing all sorts of changes and looking at my manager hoping and praying he could make more sense of them than I did. Many years on, as I led teams through the process of transformation and change, I always remembered the naïve me—worried, confused and vulnerable—so I tried to take people along the path of empathy. I started putting myself in other people's shoes before rushing to decide or judge. However, it was not always easy.

One of the toughest challenges leaders can face is driving change in their teams, whether it is in process, strategy, structure or culture. It's difficult for leaders to lead through change because they not only have to define what and how to change but also convince their teams why the change being sought is necessary. That sounds easy enough, but the problem is that different people may have different views on what kind of change is needed and whether change is needed at all. Even if a change is needed, a leader sometimes is faced with the challenge of getting their teams to embrace the change and change ways of working or thinking.

Although tough, it's a critical skill in anyone's leadership journey. In an article in June 2019 in *Forbes*, Gary Burnison, the CEO of executive search and organisational consulting firm Korn Ferry, is quoted as saying that for a leader the No. 1 predictor of success is agility—the ability to anticipate, react to and thrive in times of change.

The article was written in 2019, and while that does not seem like a long time ago, much has changed in the world since then, which has accentuated the importance of being agile and resilient through change even more. COVID-19 upended much of our lives—how we worked, how businesses operated and how people shopped and lived their lives. Through this period, the leaders who thrived were the ones who were not paralysed by the challenges posed by change but were able to rise to the challenges and navigate the changing times while taking their teams along. A report in September 2020 titled 'The Need for Speed in a Post-COVID World' by McKinsey says that organisations and leaders who were able to react with speed to changing environments significantly outperformed those who did not. They showed 3X growth and 2.5X financial performance compared to those who were slower to adapt.

I have seen that play out in recent times. I joined a new organisation at the peak of the COVID-19 pandemic, in the second half of 2020, and I began a new inning in my career without going to the office or meeting any of my teammates face-to-face. The basics of what I believed made for good leadership remained more or less the same, but the way to bring them to bear had to change radically in light of the new realities. I had to quickly adapt to, and learn and unlearn some things about effective leadership.

While it is clear that being agile is a key predictor of your leadership success and for the outcomes your team or business delivers, leading through change has its challenges, not just for the team undergoing change, but for the leader who is trying to bring about that change. The following pages give you straight answers to some common questions on leading through change.

One hundred words at a time.

We are going through a big change management project in my department, and as a team leader, I am expected to drive a lot of that change. I have been in this role for a couple of years, putting in place and being part of the teams that set up a lot of the processes and ways of working. How can I balance between doing things as before and driving change the way the management wants?

We often believe leaders create success through passion. An even stronger test is whether they can be objective enough to question their choices and tear down what they created. The balance between being passionate and detached is difficult. Perhaps, it lies in being passionate about the end but open-minded about the path, knowing that the path to success is rarely linear, and detours often lead to new opportunities. So be committed to your goals but be open to new ways of achieving them. As the Bhagavad Gita says, 'Detachment is not that you own nothing, but that nothing owns you.'

My boss said we need to have a stronger mindset to change, otherwise we will need to look at a bigger transformation project. That 'T' word scares me because when the big bosses start throwing it around, it often means restructuring and job cuts. As a team leader, how can I inspire my team to adapt to change?

'Transformation' is an often-misunderstood word as it implies restructuring, reorganisation and strategy changes, all big and infrequent events. See how you can think of change as an always-on process—transforming yourself in ways big and small, learning what works and what not, pivoting to adjust to changing realities and making choices to succeed. Often when a business needs a transformation project, it means it has failed to stay future-ready. In my journey, I have been most successful when I have a healthy dissatisfaction with the status quo and have stumbled when I became part of that status quo.

I am new in my role as a leader, and our business is going through a lot of changes and uncertainty. Some people at my workplace are reacting by doubling down on their aggression, just telling their teams what to do and being very nasty towards anyone who fails. The reality is that in an uncertain time, even leaders may not have all the answers, and I am quite sure I will make some mistakes along the way. Is that okay?

Some believe a leader needs to be an alpha individual—hungry and pushing the boundaries. To an extent, that is true, but what makes a leader great is balancing that hunger with humility. Humility keeps you from believing in your own myth, teaching you that success lies not in being infallible but in bouncing back after mistakes. Humility teaches you when to ask for help because leadership does not mean having all the answers but asking the right questions. Humility makes people follow you when the chips are down because it teaches you to earn people's trust through example, not empty words.

You are a creative person on top of being a business leader, so I suppose coming up with new ideas comes naturally to you. How can I get new ideas at my workplace? I have been told that I am analytically very strong but I do not generate enough new or 'breakthrough' ideas. What does that even mean, and can I even learn to do so?

There are many ways to generate breakthrough outcomes, but what often helps is a simple change in mindset by asking 'why not?' more often when faced with new ideas or ways of doing things versus always asking 'why?' The biggest barrier to breakthrough is getting too wedded to the status quo and constraining ideas based on what you know and are comfortable with, instead of being open to new possibilities and being curious about what you don't know. Success comes from many things—strategies, capabilities, resources, plans etc.—but often it starts with the right mindset more than anything else.

My organisation is facing some overall business challenges. My team members often give feedback about all the things we need to change, especially that the current ways of doing things are not ideal. I understand their feedback, but what is the right balance between just complaining about how things are and focusing on doing the best you can when things are not working out for your team? What can my role as a leader be in such a situation?

If you tell me you've never failed, you are either the luckiest person alive or a liar. Every team and every person fails. When your team faces challenges, there are only three things you can do as a leader—lead, follow or get out of the way. Lead with ideas if you can or, importantly, follow those who may have better ideas than yours. The worst thing you can do is complain, be negative and hold others back. Create an environment where people are comfortable talking about what needs to change, but importantly, enrol team members to help find solutions.

You have had a long and successful career. As you look back on how you have coped with challenges and changes, what is your biggest learning on sustaining success and avoiding failure?

Hindsight is wonderful; it makes successes look more deserving and failures more avoidable than they actually are. One way to beat the odds and succeed more than you fail is to never start believing in your own myth, no matter how good you think you are or how much of a winning streak you are on. Keep learning from your failures. Do not take success for granted or consider it as an entitlement. Use your experiences to try and anticipate what could go wrong. Success is often nothing more than identifying potential failure early on and preventing it from happening.

I am stepping into a new leadership role, replacing someone who was there for a few years. I can see something that is working well, but some things clearly need to change. Any advice for a new leader of a team that is going through leadership change?

Leadership changes reveal a lot about the character of leaders. Weak leaders see the past as something to 'spin', blaming problems on the old 'regime' while trying to hoard credit for successes. Strong leaders see the past as a foundation to build on, taking a balanced view of what works and where change is needed, not for their personal agenda but for their team's success. Insecure leaders seek credibility by dissing the previous 'regime' and focusing on their own image. Secure leaders never badmouth their predecessors—they focus not on themselves but on understanding and taking their new teams along.

My bosses keep saying that I need to demonstrate high potential by delivering results today, while keeping my team and business ready for tomorrow. Other than the tools and templates for long-range planning, what mindsets or attitudes do I need to develop to be a leader who can think longer-term?

Leaders who deliver today need to be competent, efficient and focused, but leaders who create tomorrow need to also be open-minded and curious. Some leaders rest on past laurels and have a fixed mindset that there is only one formula for success or one way of doing things. The successful leader has the open-mindedness to embrace new ways of doing things and the courage to challenge their own beliefs without feeling threatened. They are curious about what's changing around them and adapt to those changes. Without curiosity and open-mindedness, the competent leader of today risks becoming an obsolete leader tomorrow.

I get a sense that our business is going to be disrupted with the changes in technology and our environment. I have been trying to convince my boss that we need to change many aspects of how we do business, but he seems close-minded and believes that what has worked for us will continue to work in the future. I will continue to try and influence him, but what are your thoughts on leadership in terms of being able to anticipate and react to change?

Some leaders create change, some adapt to it and yet others have change thrust upon them. Success often comes from being aware of the changing environments—market dynamics, consumer behaviours, organisational directions etc. It also comes from being self-aware of our strengths and opportunity areas. Successful leaders use this awareness to anticipate, understand, embrace and lead change. Leaders who cling to a comfortable and familiar past, and focus on rationalising and defending it, are often the ones who find themselves becoming as obsolete as the past they are trying to cling on to, even as the world around them changes.

I have read your book on personal branding, and there are a lot of great tips in there. What, according to you, would be the most important lessons for a new leader like me, especially at a time of change and uncertainty of the sort we have been operating in since 2020?

If there's one 'superpower' you can work on to enhance your personal brand, make it adaptability. The strongest brands are those that thrive amidst changing markets and consumer behaviours and, while staying true to their core, adapt to different market needs. It is the same with our personal brands. We all have some core strengths, but they are not unidimensional. All of us have our toolboxes of skills, styles and strengths, and the best leaders are those who have the self-awareness and EQ to know which of those to flex when they work in different environments and through different challenges.

Everyone says that one of the toughest tests for a leader is to embrace and drive change. What is the toughest change or transformational challenge a leader can face?

The toughest thing for a brand to do is to obsolete itself, to change as markets and consumers change, but those are the brands that thrive. It is the same with us as leaders. It is easier to ask others to change and to say we are in favour of the change, but much tougher when we need to question our beliefs and what we have taken for granted, and to know when we need to embrace new ideas and ways of doing things. When did you last obsolete yourself or challenge your deeply held beliefs to embrace a new future?

Our business and industry are going through a whole set of changes and adapting to that change is a key priority for us as leaders. We have hired a consultant to help us through this, and I am attending training and workshops on how to lead a team through change. What else can I do to make myself a leader who is more comfortable with change?

Most leaders will talk about how important change is, but human nature is such that we are always more comfortable with others making changes than changing ourselves. However, being comfortable with change is not just something you turn on like a switch. It is a skill you can build over time, and a lot of that is in your mind. Change some habits you have had for a long time; learn a new skill outside of work; try a very different daily routine. The more comfortable you get with becoming uncomfortable, the more you will find yourself open to change.

I am a new leader who is faced with an organisational mandate to bring about some big-ticket changes in our business, for example, changing the business model and exploring fundamentally different ways of doing work, which will mean a lot of changes in how our teams need to work as well. It seems so daunting and there are so many big changes I need to make! Where do I get started?

When driving change, leaders sometimes feel frustrated because they take on the biggest challenges first. According to the domino effect principle, each small change has a multiplicative effect as each domino can knock down another one and a half times its size. So starting with a five-millimetre-tall domino, within 29 dominos, you could topple the Empire State Building! Instead of trying to drive change through one huge effort, pick a small change and get the team to taste early success. Then focus on a bigger one, then another etc. Soon you will create an unstoppable momentum leading to big changes.

We have just finished a transformational project on our business and the results are great. The project team that was working on this has been disbanded and the consultants helping us are no longer working with us. My big worry is to sustain the changes. Any ideas?

Driving significant change in a business is hard whether you are changing strategy or business models but making changes stick is even harder. Leaders sometimes focus on processes and structures to make change sustainable. They are important, but what is often most critical in making changes stick is having the right people in the team. Have a healthy mix of change agents—people who do not get complacent or satisfied with the status quo but challenge it—in the team. Empower them, give them a seat at the table and be visibly supportive of a culture of learning and experimentation.

I am trying to drive some big-process changes and transformations in my team, but we are stuck. We came up with a bunch of ideas, but none of them seems breakthrough enough individually. What do I do? Do I keep working on a bigger idea or just get started with what we have?

This is true whether you're a writer dealing with writer's block, a professional evaluating career opportunity, a businessman trying to transform results, a recruiter looking to hire the best candidate or just a person trying to better a relationship. Too much energy is often spent on getting things 'just right' and waiting for the 'perfect' solution versus continuing to move forward to challenge the status quo and to get better every day with everything you do. A lot of small steps in the right direction often take you where you want to go versus waiting for that magical, perfect leap.

As a leader, you may have helped build a lot of businesses and organisations, so I was hoping you can help me. If a business needs a lot of change, how do you deal with changing or even breaking down what you have created yourself? How difficult is it to do? What mindset should a leader build to be able to do this?

Insecure leaders personalise decisions and take questioning of their choices as a personal affront. They create a culture in which energy is spent rationalising and defending the status quo, not challenging it, and missing the point that it is not about them but about setting their businesses and people up for growth beyond their tenure. Great leaders know that their choices are a foundation of growth and change for future leaders. As in sports, records are meant to be broken, and great leaders encourage those who can improve on what they have done and not see them as a threat.

I am leading a team that is set to bring about significant transformation in the way we work. The market has changed a lot over the last few years, so has technology, and we all agree that business as usual will not deliver results in the future. Here is my dilemma. How do I define transformational success and bring about a meaningful and lasting change?

One reason leaders fail in driving lasting change is that they focus on defining transformation just by results and not in terms of mindset, capabilities and culture. A team may deliver short-term results but relapse into business as usual as soon as the transformation effort ends. Lasting transformation comes when the team embraces change, when there is an investment to support ongoing change and when the work culture is rewired to sustain transformation. It's not as simple as setting or achieving a single goal; sometimes, the challenge is to create a culture and mindset to sustain any transformation that has been achieved.

1 MILLION+ LINKEDIN VIEWS

We have recently had a leadership change, and the new leader seems hell-bent on questioning and changing everything that existed before. I do not want to sound like the guy who always defends the status quo, but I do want to make sure we do not throw the baby out with the bathwater. How do I strike that balance?

Balancing is a great skill to have for a leader, especially during times of change when the leader needs to balance between continuing what has worked and being open-minded in embracing change. The important thing is for the leader to be clear about why they are continuing or changing something. The worst reason to hold on to something is ego or inertia, and the worst reason to blindly follow change is to avoid conflict. Good leaders try to strike that balance by rooting their choices in the interests of their consumers, customers and employees and taking themselves out of the picture.

One of the biggest changes we have dealt with over the pandemic is remote working. It looks like some sort of hybrid working will remain for some time. The hardest thing about remote working is that there is no scope for the kind of relationships that we used to share by being together in office every day. How can one adapt to this change?

Whether you are in office or working from home, forming a connection is critical. In a virtual world, some of the things you can do are—call just to chat and connect with teammates, without a business or transactional agenda; while on call, never jump right away to the task at hand, but spend time checking in on each other; and finally, celebrate and get-together virtually. Keep your video on when you can; smiling, making eye contact, and positive body language are great ways to connect, whether you are in the same room or looking at each other on screens.

Everybody talks about being a 'change agent'. My bosses keep saying that we need more 'change agents'. What exactly does that mean? How does one become a change agent?

Three Cs that help develop the mindset to become a change agent are curiosity, continuous learning and courage of conviction. Curiosity is understanding the 'why' before jumping to action, seeing different sides of every story and appreciating that there are different ways of solving any issue. Continuous learning means the humility to accept that we never 'know it all' and the hunger to keep learning and improving. And finally, the courage of conviction (well, technically two Cs there!) entails challenging the status quo, accepting setbacks and persisting in moving forward versus accepting the safety and comfort of the status quo.

My company seems fond of using consultants to drive change management projects. Do consultants help or should we, as leaders, be taking much more accountability for driving change?

Some companies use consultants to help drive transformations, and good consultants can be a great help. However, a consultant does not take away the leader's responsibility to own and drive change. It is like getting a chef for a few sessions to help you learn how to cook something new. You need to have the desire to learn something new in the first place—the humility to learn new skills, the persistence to keep at it even when you've burnt the first dish and retaining that hunger for improvement to keep on cooking when the chef is no longer there.

Is it not pain when companies keep 'transforming'? One restructuring after another leaves people fatigued, insecure and dreading the next change. Is there such a thing as unhealthy change?

Constant change can seem hard for organisations. However, change, in itself, is neither good nor bad. What matters is why that change is happening. Organisations that keep changing their strategy, purpose or priority too often are perhaps changing too fast too soon without committing to anything. However, pivoting, learning and adapting to deliver a clear direction or priority is sometimes a healthy change and indeed often the hallmark of a learning organisation. Sometimes, transformational change happens when teams have a clearly aligned vision of where they want to go and are flexible and agile in adjusting how to get there.

My team needs to change, otherwise, we will not succeed. But one of the members refuses to change and seems comfortable with the way things are. How does a leader deal with team members who are resistant to change?

When dealing with team members who are not aligned to the direction of the team, start by understanding their reasons. If it is because they are not clear, enrol them. If they are afraid of failure, support them. If they are not confident, teach them. Most of the time, these will unlock commitment. There will be some people who do not want to change because they are too wedded to the status quo or are trying to protect their turf. In those situations, you do need the hard conversation whether they must be a part of the journey moving forward.

Some people have advised me that I should replace people in my team if we want to drive significant change in our business. Is that true? Does it make sense to replace all the people with a change in strategy? How should I think about this?

A change in business direction should not always mean replacing team members. Imagine a boat rowing in a new direction. It's okay if some rowers are slower or need to strengthen muscles. They need to build capabilities. If people are committed but need the capability to do certain things, leaders should invest in teaching them. However, everyone must be rowing in the same direction. That is commitment. If some are not committed to the new direction, leaders should try to enrol them. But beyond a point, it must be decided if they need to be relocated to a new boat.

People use the word transformation all the time. What exactly does that mean, and how is that different from normal, everyday change? Or is it just another fancy corporate word?

Transformation is sometimes an overused word. A key differentiator of true transformation, as against change that is more business as usual, can be found in the answers to few questions. Are your new choices forcing you to make some fundamental trade-offs or changes in how business was run in the past? Do these choices require significant changes to your team's behaviours, culture or work processes? Do these choices require capabilities to be built, which the team does not already fully have? If the answers are in the affirmative, then perhaps, the change is truly a transformational change with lasting impact.

My company is going through a huge process of change, and I am not sure I am energised by the new direction. I had joined this place hoping to make a lot of impact and drive growth. Looks like the new direction is all about protecting short-term profitability, and there are a lot of cutbacks in investments. Should I leave and do something else?

When the direction of your organisation does not resonate with you anymore, leaving it is always an option. However, before you exercise that option, ask yourself a few simple questions. Do you fully understand the intent of the change of direction? Change may be uncomfortable in the short term, but does the long-term destination appeal to you? Are your strengths and passions valued more, or less, through the change? Do you fundamentally enjoy the work culture and people you work with? All businesses go through change, therefore, do ask yourself these questions before making any career decisions based on short-term change.

1 MILLION+ LINKEDIN VIEWS

I am dealing with a change of leadership, and my new boss is nothing like the former one. While my former boss would try to get to know me and my team, and seemed to focus on growing and developing us, the new one is just so different in style and approach that I find it difficult to adjust. At a time like this, how can I cope with the change myself and simultaneously keep my team motivated?

Do not rush to conclusions just because a new leader is different from the predecessor. Often, we get comfortable with what is familiar and look at the past with rose-tinted glasses. Seek to understand the new leader's motivations, purpose and intent versus just reacting to a different style of functioning. Understand what new perspective from your boss could help your team move forward. Then combine that with what has been working in the past. The future often lies not in hanging on to the past or blindly changing for change's sake but in the thoughtful synthesis of the old and new.

I began my career almost a dozen years ago, and the reality is that the industry has changed a lot since then. Consumers and customers need change, and technology has transformed how business is done. As a leader, I find myself so caught up in internal processes, managing my team and internal stakeholders, that I fear I don't have time to stay abreast of how things are changing in the industry. Am I right in worrying that I might lose touch with how work is getting done? Any thoughts on how I could reprioritise?

Leadership should not mean losing touch with the ground realities of execution. The best generals don't just stare at maps in the war rooms; they intimately understand the battlefield's terrain from first-hand experiences. No matter where you are in your leadership journey, it is critical to prioritise spending time with those 'in the trenches' and with consumers and customers. It is easy to get caught up in corporate rituals, but as a leader, you make nothing and sell nothing personally. So you will become increasingly disconnected unless you are in step with changing realities and reflect those in your decisions.

My boss is asking whether we should change our strategy as it is not delivering the results we had hoped for. True, the results are not to our expectations, but the reality is that it has only been a few months since we implemented the strategy. However, the poor results have taken everyone by surprise and there is a lot of questioning of our direction. How do I balance between taking a hard call on changing a strategy when it is not working, and overreacting and changing direction without giving the strategy a chance to work?

When faced with failure, it is natural to start questioning the current strategy. Changing direction may be appropriate but ask three questions before doing that. First, 'why did we fail?' Was it a flawed strategy or poor execution? Second, 'what have we learnt about the capabilities we need to succeed in the future?' Third, 'how should we work differently in future to anticipate issues and react in a more agile way?' The first question can help decide whether to change direction. The next two help learn from failure and set you up for success, no matter what direction you take.

I have been in my organisation for almost a dozen years and always thought I was building a long-term career here. I had pretty much stopped thinking of what else I could do with my career. Then came some global corporate changes, and my role is being restructured. Very soon, I will find myself out of a job; and given the current state of the economy, I am not hopeful I will find another job very soon. I have never had a gap in my career, and it is freaking me out. Any advice?

A gap in your career should not mean a gap in your life. Every career journey is not linear, and sometimes, detours open up new opportunities and help us learn more about ourselves. The question is what will you do with this gap? Rethink your career direction based on what you have learnt about your passion and strengths. Build your skills by learning something new or honing current skills. Get involved in serving others—mentor someone or help with causes you care about. A gap isn't good or bad in itself—it all depends on what you fill it with.

I had been in a senior manager role at a multinational firm but had to take a break with the birth of my first child. I ended up taking a longer-than-expected break because my son had some health issues early on. Thankfully, things are much better now, and I am ready to join work again. However, I must admit to being a bundle of nerves. This is a big change after a break of almost two years. Some HR managers I spoke to initially said such a long break will work against me. I have had a couple of interviews since then, and things are moving in the right direction. But I am not sure if the organisation I join will enable me to have the kind of life I feel I need right now—a balance between career and family. What can I do to prepare myself for a successful transition?

As you ready yourself for a big transition, such as returning to work after a break, do homework on potential employers. Do not focus only on the work but understand the culture so you understand what best fits you. Build self-awareness to know what strengths you can leverage and areas you must work on. Think of your 'supporting team'. For example, how you and your spouse will divide responsibilities and support each other once you start working. Finally, be unapologetic about having taken a break! Be authentic and choose an organisation that embraces the full you, not just a resume.

My unit needs to make some basic changes in our operating strategy. With the changes in the external environment, we need to make some choices that are very different from the past. The broad team is very committed, but the change in direction is going to be a huge change for them. My boss is saying we should call a meeting of all team members to explain the changes in strategy and to make it clear what is different from the past, and what are the new expectations. Is there anything else I could do to help my team embrace and understand the change?

When making their teams follow a new direction or strategy, leaders often jump to 'what' and 'how' the team needs to work differently to deliver the goods. Often, the best buy-in happens when leaders start with the 'why', explaining as transparently as possible why the status quo is not an option for the team to achieve its ambitions and why the new direction is better. That done, the best leaders involve their teams to help craft the best way to deliver on the new direction, as it is now their shared direction versus something that only the leader is pushing.

Reflection Sheet on Leading through Change

What am I going to apply at my workplace and with my teams?

____

____

____

____

How do these questions and answers spark my mind to think differently about leading?

____

____

____

____

What additional questions do I have that are not covered here?

____

____

____

____

Leading Yourself

> 'Live as if you were to die tomorrow.
> Learn as if you were to live forever.'
>
> —Mahatma Gandhi

Leading a team, especially through a time of change, is a huge challenge for an aspiring or new leader. However, learning how to do those will not in themselves make you a great leader. To be great, you need to learn to effectively lead one additional person.

You.

The strongest leaders are often those who combine the ability to lead others with a strong sense of self-awareness and the ability to translate that self-awareness into a learning mindset. As a result, they are continuously learning and growing, becoming stronger leaders and better people. Leadership for such people is not a destination but a journey. The fallacy many young managers sometimes have is that they are waiting to 'arrive', when the reality is that no matter where you are in your career, you will get better if you continue to learn and develop yourself. In an article in August 2020 in *Forbes*, titled 'For Senior Executives, Personal Development Is Professional Development', Jenn Lofgren, a Forbes Council member, writes, 'Just because you have reached the perceived pinnacle of your career does not mean that you have reached the pinnacle of your effectiveness and impact.'

I learnt some powerful lessons in what it takes for leaders to relearn and reinvent themselves—not in a boardroom, corporate training session or executive coaching centre, but a karate dojo. I learnt karate till I was in college, attaining a brown belt. Then business school and career took precedence and it quickly disappeared from my life. I reconnected with it seven years ago after my son 'discovered' a poster in a club near our home. It was an advertisement for karate classes; he pointed out to me as he was aware that I once used to learn karate. He, too, was keen to learn.

We went up to meet Sensei Ronald Ely, and like many 6-year-old boys, my son bragged about how I once used to learn karate and became a brown belt. The sensei was, of course, happy to teach my son. He asked me whether I would want to learn again. That was not something I had on my mind, but my son's enthusiasm prevailed, and at the age of forty, twenty years after I had last been in a karate dojo, I joined my son in a class in which the next oldest student was half my age.

The sensei had one condition though—I start as a novice and work my way up from a white belt. After five years, I had worked my way back up to where I was twenty years earlier, earning my brown belt. In six years, I got my black belt. My son, who also has a black belt now, and I are still his students. Yes, we are still learning. This experience taught me more about self-growth than any amount of corporate training. It taught me that one is never too old to learn, that one should be humble enough to learn from anyone, even from someone half his age. When I was in college, a black belt was something I coveted. Today, I realise that getting a particular belt was never the destination but just a part of my learning journey.

Charting any journey involves knowing your destination and the direction you need to take, but sometimes, it helps to know exactly where you are starting from. The best leaders I have observed, worked for and learnt from, have a high sense of self-awareness. They are keenly aware of who they are and who they are not; they can bring that authenticity to what they do and play to their strengths. They also have the humility to know what they can get better at.

Growing in their careers is something that is understandably top of mind for most people in the corporate sector. Consequently, most questions I get from readers are on this topic. In answering them, I have tapped into all I have learnt, not just in my career but in my life, about what it takes to be a lifelong learner and to be on a journey of continual growth. Here are my answers to some of those questions.

One hundred words at a time.

I am a relatively new leader. When I was younger, I was confident because I studied at one of the top business schools and was doing well at work. Now I find myself surrounded by smart people, all with impressive degrees and doing well in their careers. How do I stand out here?

Many people talk about their 'profiles' in terms of degrees and roles. Those are important but you are more than the sum of your degrees and designations. In branding terms, those are often called points of parity. Demonstrate your ability and willingness to learn from your successes and failures; express your authentic self beyond how you assume people expect you to 'show up'; tap into skills you have picked up from interests outside work. You will succeed not by competence and qualifications alone but through self-awareness, learning agility and bringing your authentic self to work. Those are often the points of difference.

I have recently been promoted to a new leadership role. I have had a great run at this organisation so far and am excited at this new opportunity. My bosses tell me that I have the potential to go far and be successful here. My peers often tell me that I am the expert at what I do. While all that praise does excite me and make me confident, the reality is that I have only about six years of experience and have a long, long way to go. As you look back at your career and think of other young leaders you have seen succeed and fail, anything I should watch out for?

You should, of course, be proud of what you are capable of and what you have achieved. Just be mindful of the thin line between humility and hubris. The best way to stay grounded is to remember that everyone will have ups and downs, and the best use of a period when you are doing well is to help others with what you have learnt, keep being curious, learn new things, improve yourself, and not rest on your laurels. The road to success will have its ups and downs, but one thing that will always serve you well is humility.

I have been dealing with some issues related to a seriously ill family member. Taking care of that, along with all my responsibilities at work, is starting to take a toll on me. As a leader, I feel responsible for the team's results, and I feel guilty about taking too much time off. But I do need to be there for my family. How do I manage a balance?

If you have family, or health issues, do not assume it can be business as usual at work. Learn to ask for help when you need it rather than trying to be a martyr by attempting to do too many things. This is something I learnt later than I should have. As a leader, build empathy so that you know when your people have problems in their lives outside work and need support. Success comes not just from running faster and faster but also from having the wisdom to know when to step off the treadmill, if for a while.

I am in a dilemma regarding my career. I am working in a small firm, but I love the empowerment I get and the impact my work makes. However, I have got an offer from a much larger firm, where I suppose I will get the advantages of being in a larger set-up, but I am not sure if I will get the same level of independence. Any advice on what I should do?

Someone asked for career advice—'big fish, small pond or small fish, big pond?' Wrong question. You go round in circles in a pond. Think of it as a stream. Is it flowing in a direction you like? Will you see interesting places along the way? Will you swim with fish you like? Will there be fish who inspire you, and will you get an opportunity to help others? Will you meet and learn from diverse creatures beyond fish like you? Those are the real questions to ask, not the size of the fish or the size of the pond.

If you think about your long career and growth in the corporate sector, do you sometimes get nostalgic about how things were when you were younger? When you were younger, what did you aspire to be? Now that you are in a leadership position, does the reality match your expectation?

When you're young, you want to make your own decisions versus being told what to do. When you are older and burdened with making tough choices, you get nostalgic about your carefree youth. When you are young and people make decisions for you, remember they are just trying to do their best. Learn from decisions both good and bad, to help you when you are in their shoes. When you're older, stay in touch with your younger self so that your decisions reflect empathy for those they will impact. That is the story of 'growing up' in life and careers.

I sometimes get conflicting advice when it comes to taking risks. Some of my bosses have told me that it is best to be cautious and set modest expectations so that I can beat them and have great performance appraisals. A few have told me to think bigger and try new things. What's your take on this?

Icarus flew too high, too fast and came crashing down. One could learn from the story to be cautious and not soar too high. But what if there is another lesson? Is it better to aim for the stars, and occasionally crash and burn than never try to break the mould? It's worth thinking about in a world where everyone talks about breakthroughs but most reward and expect conformity. My two cents—we will all fall at times, but it is better to fall not because you stumbled in the mud, but you tried to soar into the sky.

By and large, I like my work. I love being around creative people and being in the thick of things when ideas are being created. However, there is a lot of administrative work that must be done as well—chasing clients for payment, and managing timelines and so on, which are not nearly as much fun! My boss keeps piling up the administrative work, and whenever I tell him that I would love to get more exposure to the creative side as I grow, he seems to just focus on the work he needs me to get done here and now. Any advice on how to think about this and whether I am working in the right place and for the right boss?

In any job, there will be times when you have to do things not because you love doing them but because the reality of life and work is such that stuff sometimes needs to get done. However, when you think of who you would want to be around, don't just look at how they reward you for things that have to be done. See if they understand, nurture and value what you love. The former means they value you as a resource to get things done now; the latter means they value you as a person long term. Big difference.

I am new to leading teams, and I have never got a clear and straight answer to one question—whether it is more important to be smart or hard-working, to be successful as a leader. What are the critical traits to be a successful leader and which of them is more important if I want to be successful?

One of my team members once asked me the same question—smartness or hard work? The honest answer is that it depends. Sometimes you need to cut through the clutter and simplify, at other times you need to dig in and work hard. Success lies not in being one or the other but in being able to adapt to circumstances. I added that perhaps the most important thing is to have integrity. IQ and hard work will all be undone if people don't trust you and if you are motivated only by your success versus genuinely trying to help others.

Leading a team is hard work! I get so caught up in doing my work, supervising my team, checking on what they need etc., that I hardly seem to have any time or energy left for things outside of work. Is this part and parcel of being a leader or am I missing something?

I have found that there is a resource a leader needs to manage carefully, one that most leadership trainings do not cover. Energy. This is a key skill leaders must have to keep up with demanding expectations, do justice to the many roles they are expected to play and yet not burn out or have health issues. This means being clear on priorities (knowing what to focus on), being disciplined (knowing when to dive in and when to delegate or let go), ensuring sufficient 'downtime' versus being 'always on' and having ways to recharge (time with family, hobbies or exercise).

1 MILLION+ LINKEDIN VIEWS

Today is Teachers' Day. In your long career, who or what have you learnt the most from? Who has been your most important teacher?

My most important teacher has been failure—failures at work (failed initiatives, bad decisions and poor people choices) and in personal life (things I regret saying and doing, relationships I messed up, and things left unsaid and undone). They have taught me much—to be humble, to accept my imperfections but be hungry for improvement, to be aware of my limitations but be inspired to keep pushing them, and the realisation that success is not being in the spotlight yourself but when you help others shine. As you celebrate teachers, celebrate your own failures and what they have taught you.

They say it is lonely at the top. It is one of the things that makes being a senior leader seem less aspirational than I may have expected. Is it true that as you get more senior, you must deal with your own problems and that you start getting lonely? What have you experienced as you climbed the corporate ladder?

Is it lonely at the top? It is as lonely as you want it to be. As a young leader, I made the mistake of dealing with problems alone, thinking asking for help equalled weakness. I have learnt that strong leaders can also be vulnerable, which makes them authentic and relatable. When dealing with tough issues in business, career or personal life, reach out to those you can trust or help, such as co-workers, bosses, mentors, family and friends. You may soar high, but you need not feel lonely, because we can all be the wind beneath each other's wings.

I used to work for a leader who always made me uncomfortable because he would keep talking about how we must not blindly follow the rules and know when to bend them. The problem was that some of my peers took this as a license to do unethical things, which I was never okay with, and that is part of the reason I left to join a new organisation. What is your take on 'bending the rules'?

When under pressure or to drive business, one may be tempted to 'bend the rules' or 'push the envelope'. While good leaders always encourage considered risk-taking, they must also learn to draw the line and have the courage of conviction to take short-term business hits without compromising on doing the right thing. Leaders can bounce back from bad business decisions, bad results and bad luck, but it is very hard to bounce back when you lose the credibility and respect of those around you and, importantly, of yourself, because under pressure, your actions betray the lack of a moral compass.

I have had a pretty good run as a leader in my current organisation, and a lot of my work has been recognised by senior management. Now I've got some bad news to share. An ambitious initiative I was working on has hit some significant roadblocks, and I can only imagine how my senior management will react to this news. How do I share bad news?

If you want to build credibility as a leader, share bad news as fast as, if not faster than, good news. Many leaders spark off congratulatory message chains when things are going well but maintain radio silence when there are setbacks. Everyone sees through it, so your credibility takes a hit. Share good news and celebrate, but also share bad news, what you've learnt from the setback, how you will bounce back and any help you need. Lasting success doesn't come through cheerleading alone but by building resilience, continuous learning, asking for help when needed, and building trust and credibility.

As a leader, you need to think about the long term as a big priority. That is what my boss told me when I took on my first big leadership role. I suppose to an extent that is true for the business, but what is your take on leaders thinking and planning for the long term versus taking the time to do things that matter here and now?

Leaders are supposed to plan long term but speaking as someone who has learnt the hard way how unpredictable life can be, learn to savour the here and now. Have grand long-term plans, but do not leave things unsaid and undone if you can. Do not wait for occasional breaks to re-energise; seek energy every day by doing full justice to the roles you play at work and outside. Appreciate someone every day. Teach something every day. Learn something every day. Make a positive impact every day. You may have plans for tomorrow, but today is all you really have.

I am in a leadership role that involves influencing my peers and other stakeholders. It is sometimes challenging because everyone has their own agenda and priorities. I do try and share what is on my find but sometimes those I am trying to influence have either already made up their minds or are no longer receptive. Any tips on how to get better at influencing?

Influencing is an important skill. The mistake some managers make is to assume it has to do only with what they say (insights, information, etc.) and how they say it. Those are critical, but what many managers miss is the importance of 'when'. When are your stakeholders likely to be most receptive? When is it too late to influence them? You might have brilliant insights but if you stay silent in important interactions where decisions are being made or decision-makers are making up their minds, you miss an opportunity. Speak up, speak well but also know when to do it.

I used to have a manager who would make me spend hours 'prettying' up slides and 'massaging' numbers to find just that soundbite that would make him look good in front of his bosses. It used to drive me crazy! Now I am a team leader myself, and I cringe at the thought of getting my team members to do that kind of thing. However, sometimes I wonder if those are important leadership roles. What would you say?

Beware of leaders who make people do things 'for optics' or to 'make things look good for management'. They are really trying to make themselves look good and using their people to help push their personal agendas versus doing what good leaders ought to do—focus on what really matters for the business and the growth of their people. When faced with such leaders, try and push back. Ask how the 'work' adds up to the priorities. Sometimes, you may not be able to avoid it, but at least learn what not to do when you are in their shoes.

I am going to be presenting to our CEO for the first time, and I am a bundle of nerves. How do I react to what she says? Should I agree with whatever she offers by way of suggestions? What if she pokes dozens of holes in my work? How does one read the mind of a senior leader?

Here is an insight for those trying to read their leader's mind. Savvy leaders are wary of people in their teams who nod passively and agree to everything they say—praise or criticism. Being an echo chamber for your leader does nothing for your credibility. If there is praise coming your way, build on that success and take it to the next level. If your work is criticised, question to understand why, clarify expectations, challenge constructively and make changes as needed. When good leaders offer inputs, they are not seeking validation; they are reinforcing desired behaviours or are seeking change.

I am at a crossroads in my career. Several of my colleagues have jumped over to a new sector because it is booming (they say) and there are many more growth opportunities. They keep asking me to move as well. The problem is that I like my work and the people I am working with, and from what I hear, the culture of the place they are at is very different, even though growth prospects may be better. How should I think about this?

Many young managers have clarity on what they want to do but are less clear on the why. Lasting success comes not just from chasing something because others are doing it or because a sector or organisation is growing or attractive. It requires marrying that with a clear understanding of one's passions, strengths and the culture of the place. Understanding that helps you appreciate not just how attractive something is, but whether it is a good fit for you. Competence helps get you a job, but what will keep you there successfully over the long term is a great fit.

I have been doing well in my career, getting promoted and so on. Now, I occasionally find myself low on energy, wondering if I am doing the right thing or not. I wonder if I would be better served working in another organisation where I can have a better work-life balance, even though it might mean a lateral move as opposed to promotion. Is it normal to have doubts about where I am headed?

Many enjoy the fast pace of corporate life and its adrenaline rush. It's okay to step back occasionally to check if you're running fast—but, in fact, are stuck on a treadmill—or heading somewhere you want to go? You will find lasting fulfilment when you are headed in a direction that rings true to you, even if it means taking the occasional detour rather than always moving forward linearly at a constant pace. So there's nothing wrong with stepping back, introspecting, balancing different aspects of your life and deciding whether you do indeed want to change direction.

I am preparing for a presentation to our CEO. It's a big deal, as you can imagine. I have been spending a lot of time getting all my content right, having sheets of backup data and so on. Anything else I can do to make a big impact through this presentation?

When you're presenting to a group, are you inspiring, engaging and/or provoking them, or are you making people tune out? The content is important, but so is how you deliver it. Research made famous by Professor Albert Mehrabian of UCLA showed that body language and tone of voice had more impact on how we perceive messages than the words themselves. So next time you're prepping for a big meeting, go through slides and numbers, but also think through the emotion you want to elicit—your tonality, posture and body language. They all contribute significantly towards creating the impact you want.

When I was younger and starting my career, I thought the things that differentiated me from others were my college (one of the best) degree, academic pedigree and analytical skills. Now that I have spent a few years in my career and am surrounded by people with similar qualifications and skills, what can differentiate me?

Those still on campus or new to the world of work sometimes think that their degrees are what will lead them to success. The truth is that in branding terms, your degree is a 'point of parity', something most people around you contending for the same opportunities as you will have. To unlock your potential, you need to find your points of difference, the things that uniquely make you who you are. Quite often, those are rooted in things well beyond your degree, like your ability to work with people, to bounce back from failure and to adapt to change.

When I was a younger manager, I would keep hearing senior leaders talk about performance versus potential. Now that I am a leader myself, how should I approach the duality, both in terms of a career prospect and a desire to help team members understand the difference?

A common mistake among young managers is to assume that just delivering results entitles them to advancement. Results are critical, but often a 'hygiene factor'. When considering candidates with similar results, leaders often pick the one with a stronger potential, as shown through points of difference like curiosity, adaptability, teamwork and capacity to deal with ambiguity. Rather than feel aggrieved, managers would do well to embrace the fact that their personal brand is not defined by a single number but by their overall impact on results here and now, and also by demonstration of their potential to grow beyond current roles.

I read somewhere that you have had some great mentors who have helped you in your career. I have had a couple of seniors I reached out to for advice once in a while, but never really had anyone I would formally consider a mentor. If I do ask someone to be my mentor, what is the best way to get value from him/her?

Be inspired by and learn from mentors, but don't assume you need to do as they had done. Each one of us is unique, and you create the most fulfilling career when you walk a path that uniquely works for you, as against blindly following in someone's footsteps. When seeking advice from mentors, don't ask them what you should do. Ask them what questions they would have asked if they were in your situation. Mentors add the most value when you learn what questions to ask and find answers that work for you, as against relying on them for answers.

Towards the beginning of my career, it was clearer what success meant to me—my individual results and progress. Now as a leader, I am responsible for others in my team. How may I think of redefining what success means?

The most iconic brands do not just chase short-term profits but have a deeper purpose, often rooted in making a broader positive impact. What is your 'brand purpose'? The key to a successful and fulfilling career often lies in defining why you do what you do, not in terms of personal success alone but in terms of the broader impact you have on others. Helping your people shine, getting involved in the community, solving consumer issues are all potential ways to achieve your goal. A strong brand purpose leads to a lasting success and consumer satisfaction. It is the same with leadership.

I have read your book *Brand New Start* in which you lay down the importance of building a strong personal brand. I am an introvert, so I am not comfortable pushing myself in the spotlight. Is there any hope for someone like me to succeed as a leader?

Some people reject personal branding as they feel uncomfortable 'selling' themselves as products or coming across as being 'pushy'. Learn from the most iconic consumer brands that stand the test of time. They don't 'push'. Instead, they 'pull' consumers towards them by being empathetic, relevant and adding value to their lives. Similarly, building a strong personal brand has nothing to do with being 'pushy'. If anything, the most compelling leaders are people who 'pull' others towards them by helping them grow, succeed and add value to others' lives. Pull usually trumps push in the world of brand building and leadership.

As a new leader, my head sometimes spins when looking at the lists of competency and success factors that the HR department says is important for a leader to succeed in our organisation. Then there are all the functional and business aspects I need to know. To be a good leader, am I expected to be well-versed in all of them?

Growing up in a middle-class Indian family, I would hear from relatives about how it was best to be an 'all-rounder', someone good at everything—academics, sports, behaviour etc. To create authentic and compelling leadership, it's sometimes better not to be an all-rounder but to have a few jagged edges. Nobody can be good at or passionate about everything. Pick a few things that make you tick and play to your strengths and be awesome at them, instead of trying to tick every box. Brands succeed by having a few sharp differentiators, instead of trying to be everything to everyone.

I am trying to get better at communication as a leader because I have been told that it would help me improve my executive presence and impact. My HR leader has suggested I enrol in a workshop to build my communication skills. What else can I do to work on this?

Great brands aren't built through occasional flashes of inspiration, but by working on the fundamentals, day in and day out, in a process of continuous improvement. It's the same with communication. Don't stop at one workshop. Take the learnings and apply them every single day and seek out opportunities to learn and improve every day and in every interaction. If I may draw a parallel with my life, it's the same with karate. Discipline and practice build muscle memory, and after a point, what you project is no longer even a conscious effort but a natural extension of who you are.

Some of my peers are 'all business'. All they talk about is work and people at work. I used to have a bunch of different interests outside of work, but ever since I got promoted to a leadership position, I sometimes wonder if it is okay or not to keep indulging in them or should I also just focus on work like some of these guys?

We sometimes label ourselves and others, and a common mistake is to limit our identity by narrowly defining it in terms of where we work or our job titles. They are all components of who we are, but they don't define us. Embrace other aspects of life outside work, such as interests and passions, to define yourself broadly. Far from being a 'distraction', this alternative source of identity often helps you connect the dots you may not otherwise know, bring differential thinking to the workplace, show up in a more authentic and differentiated way and have a broader leadership impact.

As a leader, it can feel like my day starts and ends without getting a breather or realising where time went—meetings after meetings and tasks after tasks, and at the end of the day, there are a bunch of things I still need to think about or attend to, both at work and home, but I just do not have the time for that. How do you deal with this?

We get so busy 'doing stuff'—priorities, meetings and ticking off to-do lists—that we under-appreciate the power of doing nothing. Block some time in your calendar to do nothing but get in touch with how you feel, re-acquaint yourself with your identity outside of work, sort through issues bothering you or just re-energise. For me, it's my ninety-minute run every morning when I blank out everything related to work and do nothing but think about the many things I would not get the time for once the workday starts. Why don't you try blocking some time for 'doing nothing'?

I have been in the corporate world for a few years, and I notice that sometimes people just try and become clones of each other. Everyone speaks the same way, uses the same ways of presenting material and so on. I used to be great at design, and sometimes I feel that injecting some of those skills into my presentations would make them more impactful versus just dumping a bunch of numbers on them, as my colleagues do. I am passionate about design, and often I feel my work would be so much more compelling if I could bring my ideas to life more visually. Should I bring that aspect of my life into the workplace?

When it comes to communication, great leaders don't deliver impact by just sharing information and numbers. Anyone can do that. Rather, they infuse their communication with emotional impact. You might achieve success by sharing facts, like everyone else, but a way to differentiate yourself is to bring your passions and unique skills to bear on others. People can see your strengths reflect in what you deliver, but they will feel your passion in how you deliver them. So, absolutely, take what you are passionate about and good at, and inject that into your work if you can.

I have been working for close to ten years, and now I am literally on autopilot mode, so much so that when I meet any stranger, I introduce myself as working with my company. I read your book *Brand New Start*, and it provoked my thought. If my personal brand and identity are not just defined by where I work, how do I introduce myself?

Many people introduce themselves, even in non-work settings, by their workplace and their designation. That is just an aspect of our lives, not our only identity. By narrowly identifying ourselves essentially with our job profiles, we struggle to define ourselves without our jobs, which does a lot of injustice to other aspects of our lives. Before my first novel was published, I would introduce myself to strangers as an aspiring novelist. Those conversations—talking about my writing and their encouragement—often helped me keep the faith, despite mounting rejection slips. Tap into your passions outside work and ask yourself how you would introduce yourself?

You are a storyteller, and I have read some of your posts on how powerful storytelling can be in the corporate world as well. What kind of stories should one tell to motivate teams?

The stories we tell shape the leadership impact we have on others. Whether it is your kids at home or teams at work, do not just tell stories that focus on your successes. Talk about when you made bad choices, when you struggled against the odds, when you had no clue of what to do, when you took leaps of faith. Showing your vulnerability—acknowledging that you do not always have all the answers and highlighting the struggles behind the successes—builds a more authentic leadership impact and encourages those around you to do the same. What stories do you tell?

I am in an exciting phase of my career. I have been doing well in my organisation and recently got promoted into a role where I am leading a team. One thing I have learnt is to keep playing to my strengths. The role I am in plays to a lot of my core strengths, and I can see myself doing very well here. I have read some of your posts where you talk about the importance of playing to one's strengths. Are there any watch-outs while doing that?

Brands sometimes overstretch and fail because they try to extend what they do well too far. It is the same with our careers. Our strengths often hold the seeds of our darker sides, and if not used in a calibrated manner, they can also lead us to failure. Confidence can become hubris, collaboration can become an inability to say no and mastery of the present can close our eyes to imagining the future. The best way to guard against this is to stay humble, keep seeking feedback, have a learning mindset and have people around you who will keep you grounded.

1 MILLION+ LINKEDIN VIEWS

I see people posting all kinds of stuff on social media, and a lot of it just seems like they are bragging or showing off. But then, maybe that is just me! Does self-promotion really help someone build their career and personal brand? Am I missing out on something by not doing it?

Iconic brands are not built by opportunistic promotions, but by the constancy of purpose and serving consumers over the long term. It is the same with your personal brand. Do not do things just for image-building, do not take yourself too seriously and do not start believing in your own myth. Do what you do only if you genuinely care about them and want to make an impact through your ideas and actions. Sustained service and positive impact on others are what builds an authentic and sustainable career, not focusing on self-promotion or narcissism. How has serving others enriched your career journey?

As someone who is driven to succeed and has largely done well at academics and in the early phase of my career, it is tough to face failure. That is what is happening to me at work, where I have just faced a big setback. How do I deal with failure and not let it destroy my confidence in myself?

The most iconic brands have their share of failed launches. It is the same with our careers. A failure, at work or in our personal lives, should not derail us or make us lose faith. Like strong brands that stand the test of time, we need to reflect on the lessons learnt, introspect on what could have been done differently, and emerge stronger and open to the next opportunity. It's hard, but failures often open our minds to new ideas and give way to welcome opportunities that may have otherwise been missed. What did you learn from your last failure?

I have heard that being able to take risks and try new things are some of the qualities to becoming a stronger leader. How can one think about that? What questions can I ask myself to see if I am in the right direction of becoming one?

Successful brands do not rest on their laurels but test how far they can stretch, even if that means taking a risk. It's the same with leadership. Staying within our comfort zone can limit our growth. It is when we are open-minded, embrace new experiences and take leaps of faith that we learn and grow the most. A young brand manager once told me that unless an idea frightened him, it was not pushing the envelope enough. I have found that to have broad applicability. When was the last time you stepped out of your comfort zone?

I have always been very ambitious—always thinking of how I can get to the next level and grow in my career. With the pandemic, my career took a big twist. The role I was doing was no longer needed in the company, and I find myself doing a role in which I am learning some new things but I am a bit disappointed as it is a parallel move and not the upwards move that I had hoped for. Am I right in being disappointed?

It's good to be goal-driven, but it is important to learn from and enjoy the journey. That is something my sensei drilled into me. You never 'arrive' no matter what belt you wear. You are always a student—learning, humble and on a journey of self-improvement. I was a brown belt at seventeen and then restarted learning Karate at forty, starting from the bottom as a white belt. The best journeys are not linear, and sometimes, detours make you learn the most about yourself and what you truly seek. As you focus on your goals, embrace the journey—detours and all.

I am a new leader in a new role, and while I thought I was good at what I did, here I find myself surrounded by people who seem to be so much better qualified and experienced than me. My peers have been working in this sector for years and know the technical details of the industry far better than I do. My strengths, on the other hand, are more in the area of marketing and communications. How can I stand out in such a situation?

Great leaders see possibilities in what they have and make the most of them, as against focusing on what they lack. We spend too much time on what we aren't good at or comparing ourselves to others. Shift the focus. Understand what you're uniquely good at and passionate about, and make them a force multiplier, unlocking success in a way that uniquely fulfils you. You will think having wings is useless if you see them as dead weight, holding you back in a race in the dirt. But you will think otherwise when you realise that you were born to fly.

I am a team leader in a new organisation; I succeeded someone who was in this role for many, many years. My predecessor was good at the role, but his style and way of working were very different from my natural style. For example, he would be very formal and hierarchical while I try and be much less so. Should I change my style to fit into how this team and organisation have run in the past?

Teachers, parents and bosses often overstate the importance of conformity. In the world of branding, your brand needs to stand out and be differentiated to thrive. Certainly, understand and adapt to the points of parity of your environment, that is, the hygiene factors, but you will never shine if all you do is walk in someone else's shadow. The core quality of a successful leader is understanding what uniquely makes you tick, and injecting that authentic and unique self into whatever you do. Leaders who truly leave a legacy do not spend their lives trying to fit into a mould; they break it.

I used to be great friends with my colleagues. We used to chat about all kinds of things, and they were my support system in a way. Now that I have been promoted into a leadership role, I obviously cannot share with them a lot of what is on my mind when it comes to professional matters. Does getting to higher levels of leadership make you lonelier? How do you find people you can turn to for advice when you need it?

Building authentic and compelling leadership is not a solitary pursuit. Seek help from those around you; create your own 'advisory board'. Cultivate trustworthy mentors to guide you. I have been lucky to have some amazing mentors. We all need confidants with whom we can share our dreams and concerns, who accept us for who we are and who help keep us grounded. For me, that is my wife, Puja, and a few close friends. Finally, do not hang out only with people like you. You learn the most when you are exposed to diverse thinking. Who is your advisory board?

The last one year has been tumultuous for my career. With the pandemic, my organisation went through a bunch of changes, and while I am lucky to still have my job, I am not sure I am enjoying my new role as much as I used to enjoy the previous one. I keep asking myself if I should take my career in a different direction that better fits my passions. I have been reading some books and talking to friends to understand what I am missing and how to act on it. Any suggestions?

Everyone needs help with rebooting or rethinking career choices, and often we reach out for help. Some read self-help books while others turn to mentors and friends for advice. Those can be helpful, but one thing that usually helps the most is taking a moment to get off the treadmill to look deep inside to get in touch with oneself. To unlock career breakthroughs, understand your passions, motivations and strengths; crystalise those into a purpose-driven plan, as against just chasing designations and packages; and finally, be mindful of 'fit' instead of chasing someone else's definition of success.

I am in a new role and a bit of a bind. There is another leader I need to work with closely since our teams have to work collaboratively. He is always focused on who reports to whom and who controls which budget. He claims that this is important to have control over his business. He has been doing this much longer than I have, and I wonder if he is right.

Some managers obsess about their 'turf'—budgets, reporting lines and ways of working. In the short term, such territoriality may well make them feel stronger or may stroke their egos, but in the long term, it can be a self-fulfilling prophecy. By holding on so tight to what they have, they inadvertently give off a signal of limited potential or the inability to take on broader roles. One of the mental transitions from being a manager to truly showing leadership potential is to think and say 'we' more than 'me' and to build bridges, as against hunkering down in your own little silo.

I have been working for several years, and every presentation to pitch an idea seems to take away some of the fun of coming up with ideas because so much of the focus goes into making slides rather than ideating. You are a writer. What lessons or tips would you share in terms of how we can share ideas with others in a more impactful way?

In the corporate world, being complex is sometimes confused with being impactful, so people default to complicated slide decks to communicate ideas. Here's a learning from my 'night job'—clarity, simplicity and emotional resonance count the most in a so-called elevator pitch when you have literally minutes to sell your idea to an agent or producer. Here's a challenge. Next time you pitch an idea at work, try and explain it within a couple of minutes with no slides. Slides are an aid, but the power of big ideas comes through when they are presented simply—with passion and conviction.

I am looking at how to steer my career and continue growing and learning. How should I think about options that come my way? I have an opportunity before me, which is a big jump from my present position, but I am not sure where it will lead in the long term. Any advice?

Don't evaluate career opportunities only by how they compare to your current reality. That's important, but it means your frame of reference is always incremental and short term. Ask where an opportunity may lead in the future. Does it open new doors through new experiences or exposure? Does it close any doors? If you are successful in this role a few years down the line, imagine the future! These not only equip you with questions you can ask your recruiter instead of just comparing to current reality but build the habit of thinking long term about your career.

A part of the challenge I have to face as a new leader is to effectively influence stakeholders, including senior leaders. In big presentations, I often have all the facts and data, but I struggle to get through to them, and get them to understand and agree with what I am trying to convey. What could I be missing?

A common mistake is to think of communication as only information sharing. That is why so many corporate presentations are basically an overload of tables, charts and facts, and the focus is on overwhelming the audience with data. However, the most impactful communication is often one that not just transmits facts but uses them to trigger emotions. Next time you are making a presentation, do not focus just on what information you are trying to share but how you want your audience to feel. Information sharing leads to intellectual head nods. However, emotional buy-in leads to commitment, conviction and trust.

1 MILLION+
LINKEDIN VIEWS

I am doing well in my current organisation, and my manager is telling me that there may be a role for me in another country. It is a wonderful role and would be great for my career, but I am really hesitating to tell him that I may have second thoughts. I am genuinely in a dilemma. At the life stage I am in, this move would mean a lot of compromises for my family, and while I would be very open to such a move after a couple of years, right now it is not ideal from a personal standpoint. How can I resolve such dilemmas?

As you grow in your career, it is natural to be faced with trade-offs. For example, a wonderful career opportunity may not be ideal for your family. Everyone must make their own choices at such times, but here are some things I have learnt. Be clear on your priorities. Do what works for you versus choosing a path just because others have done so, seek to maximise not just a unidimensional view of success but by asking what will lead to overall fulfilment in your life and, finally, be transparent and enrol others in your decision-making process, at work and home.

I have always heard that it is helpful to have mentors guide you in your journey. However, I have also heard that mentor-mentee relationships need to be a win-win. The benefits for a mentee are obvious, but what is in it for the mentor? I have sometimes hesitated to reach out to potentially great mentors because I was unsure of the benefits for them. There is no tangible gratification for them, and I do not want to impose on them. How should I be thinking about this?

Don't hesitate to approach someone who could be a great mentor because you are wondering what is 'in it' for them. Many people want to help others grow just to pay it forward and help others benefit from the experiences and lessons they have picked up, often from mentors of their own. A 'win' need not be any material or tangible benefit-forming relationship; the joy of helping someone and knowing you have made a positive impact on them are all considered wins. It is not about gratification. Those who are passionate about mentoring are motivated by things beyond that.

How does one realistically find a good mentor? I mean, people are busy and people are selfish. Everyone is out for their own success. Is it even realistic to expect anyone to truly mentor someone? I have reached out to a couple of senior leaders when I needed help with my job transitions, but that did not lead to any real mentoring from them. I am getting a bit cynical about this whole business of mentoring.

I have benefitted from some amazing mentors, and I hope I have in turn been able to mentor some people. Some thoughts for you are as follow. First, mentors do not always wear business suits. Among my best mentors have been my grandfather, my parents and my sensei. Have an open mind on whom you can learn from. Second, reach out not only for immediate benefits and transactional gains. The best mentors are those who genuinely want to build relationships and help people grow. Asking a senior leader for help in getting a job is not mentoring. Invest in long-term relationships and genuine learning.

I believe that personal growth is important in a broad sense, that is, not just in terms of career progression. I envy those who pursue their passions or hobbies in addition to their career. I used to love painting, for example, but with the demands of the job, the time I need to give to family and all the other demands that come up in day-to-day life, such as meeting friends, chores and so on, I never seem to get any time for myself and my hobbies. You have built a successful corporate career, and you seem to have the energy and time to keep writing as well. How do you manage and how can I learn to start making time for my passions as well?

Whenever someone asks me how I do all that I do—writing and a corporate career—they don't see what I choose not to do. I focus on a few passions: family, people at work counting on me, writing, fitness and giving back. Beyond that, I declutter my life. For example, I don't drink, I don't go to parties, I don't network a lot, etc. Not to say that you should do the same, but identify a few things you are passionate about, focus your energy on them and be mindful about what you are choosing not to do.

If one has a great career opportunity but is hesitant to take it up because the family is not in favour of it at that moment, how does one deal with such a dilemma? On the one hand, you want to do what your family is comfortable with, but on the other, will a part of you not regret letting a great career opportunity get away?

The best way to deal with such a dilemma is to *not* artificially compartmentalise career and family. They both contribute to making up your life, so think of it as a life decision. What's better for your life as a whole? Do the career benefits outweigh family apprehensions or would you want to prioritise what your family wants, even if it means that it's not ideal for your career? Every person will have their own answer and that answer will change over time, and across different life stages. What is important is to think of such decisions in an integrated way.

Being in the corporate world has its rewards, but it also has its share of stress and pressure. Any thoughts on how I could prevent that from getting to me? I certainly do not want to burn out along the way.

Don't be a 'corporate martyr', and if you are a leader, stop encouraging your people to be martyrs—employees who never take leave, work late, are always-on, have packed calendars and feel righteous about it. This leads to nothing more than burnout and leaves insufficient time for family or other priorities. Take time off unapologetically and be mindful of your health and energy. I am pretty balanced, but there are times I need to course-correct and remind myself that I will go further if I pace myself, taking breathers, versus sprinting all the time and running out of steam.

You have learnt karate for many years and hold a black belt. What lessons from karate do you think have broader applicability in building a career in the corporate world or succeeding in life?

As a kid learning karate, I thought confidence came from knowing how to hit. Years later, after hundreds of sparring bouts and blows in the dojo, helping my son learn karate and earn his own black belt, I know now that confidence comes not from knowing how to hit but from losing the fear of getting hit. It is the same in life and career. You succeed not just by learning how to succeed but by embracing failure. By not hiding your scars but wearing them as badge of honour—showing you can take hits, learn from them and emerge stronger.

How do you think one can define success in a corporate career? So many people talk of it as climbing the corporate ladder. Is there another way of thinking about it?

Why do we talk of success as 'climbing the corporate ladder'? It implies that there is only one possible direction for success, and the only way to go is up or down, not sideways. Careers, and life in general, should not only be about climbing the ladder because others do. They shouldn't be about chasing success as defined by others but finding personal fulfilment. Fulfilment comes from finding a path that works for you, exploring various paths along the way, and enjoying and learning from diverse experiences, as against being restricted by the corporate ladder.

Reflection Sheet on Leading Yourself

What am I going to apply at my workplace and with my teams?

How do these questions and answers spark my mind to think differently about leading?

What additional questions do I have that are not covered here?

A Parting Request

> 'When you learn, teach. When you get, give.'
>
> —Maya Angelou

This book draws to a close, but I hope our conversation does not end here. I hope that this book has been of some use to you, if not in sharing all the answers you might have been seeking, at least in stimulating you to ask the right questions. Do share any feedback you have, and of course, do send in any more questions on leadership you encounter as you grow in your leadership journey. The easiest way to get in touch with me is through my website, www.mainakdhar.com or my LinkedIn profile at https://www.linkedin.com/in/mainakdhar/. I'll try and answer any questions you have through my #leadershipin100words posts and incorporate them in the future editions of this book.

However, do not stop there. I have one small additional parting request for you.

If you find this book useful, if it helps you think differently about your leadership journey, even if in a small way, do me a big favour.

Pay it forward.

A big reason I can connect with you through this book is that I have been lucky to have learnt from many amazing mentors in my life. As you learn and grow as a leader, do not stop at defining success as purely your own growth and success.

Redefine it as helping others succeed.

Become a mentor.

That does not mean you have to know it all or have a certain amount of grey hair. Mentoring is for everyone, as what makes our lives, and our leadership journeys fulfilling is the opportunity to learn from each other.

Find your Telemachus.

Help him or her find their inner voice.

Encourage and inspire them to venture out on their own adventure.

Help them ask the questions that will make them leaders and mentors themselves.

Then you will have truly experienced the joy of leadership.

INDEX

ABOUT THE AUTHOR

Mainak Dhar wears many hats. Of all the roles he plays, he considers being a good husband and father as the most important. An alumnus of the Indian Institute of Management Ahmedabad, Mainak has worked in the corporate sector for over 25 years. He began his career with Procter & Gamble, spending 18 years in marketing and general management roles across the Asia-Pacific region. He then moved to General Mills as CEO for India and took on broader responsibilities for Asia, Middle East and Africa regions. He is currently the vice president and managing director for India and South Asia at a leading consumer products multinational.

A self-described 'cubicle dweller by day and writer by night', when not with family or at work, Mainak loves creating and sharing stories. He is the author of over 20 books, some of which have been bestsellers in India and abroad, including *Alice in Deadland*, *03:02* and *Sniper's Eye*. His books have been translated into Turkish, Vietnamese, Japanese, French, German, Hindi and Portuguese, reaching millions of readers worldwide, and two of his novels are under development as web series. His last non-fiction book, *Brand New Start: Fast-Start Your Career with the Power of Personal Branding*, was an Amazon bestseller and won Gold at the Non-Fiction Book Awards, 2021.

Learn more about him and contact him at www.mainakdhar.com.